YA
796.046
Ext

Extreme!

CLARK PUBLIC LIBRARY

3 9502 00132 5760

Y0-CCO-636

Clark Public Library
303 Westfield Ave.
Clark, NJ 07066
(732)388-5999

EXTREME!

The Ultimate Guide to Action Sports

TRIUMPH
B O O K S
CHICAGO

Contributors

**Keith Carlsen, Chris Dixon,
Jeff Erdmann, Aaron George,
Gabe Sullivan, Lynda Twardowski**
Writers

**AP/Wide World Photo,
Allsport, Kieth Carlsen,
Anthony Scavo/SportPics**
Photography

Linc Wonham ... Editor
Ray Ramos ... Designer

This book is not sponsored, authorized,
endorsed by, or otherwise affiliated with any
person featured within this book. This is not
an official publication.

Copyright © 2002 by Triumph Books

No part of this publication may be reproduced,
stored in a retrieval system, or transmitted, in
any form by any means, electronic, mechani-
cal, photocopying, or otherwise, without the
prior written consent of the publisher, Triumph
Books, 601 S. LaSalle St., Suite 500, Chicago,
Illinois, 60605.

This book is available in quantity at special
discounts for your group or organization.
For further information, contact:

**Triumph Books
601 South LaSalle Street
Suite 500
Chicago, Illinois 60605
(312) 939-3330
Fax (312) 663-3557**

Printed in the United States of America

ISBN: 1-57243-535-6

YA
796.046
EXT
2-3-07

Clark Public Library - Clark, N.J

Contents

Feel the Rush

Just what the hell is "extreme" anyway? Is it a crew of morons chugging Mountain Dew before hucking themselves off a cliff on snowboards, skis, or mountain bikes? Is it Laird Hamilton towing into an 80-foot wave at Jaws? Tony Hawk pulling a 900 before a crowd of delirious fans? Travis Pastrana pulling his 100th backflip on a souped-up Suzuki? Uberskier Shane McConkey base jumping off the roof of the Mandalay Bay hotel in Las Vegas?

Undoubtedly, all of those things qualify as extreme. But maybe, just maybe, extreme is also something a little bit simpler.

When I was ten years old I watched my nine-year-old cousin bust out all his front teeth after pulling a faceplant on his G&S Fibreflex skateboard. When he gaped up at me with a shattered, bloody mouth, I remember thinking, "Now *that* was extreme."

When I was about 11 I watched my buddy, Jay Burns, pull his first serious air on a Rampar BMX bike. Today, 25 years later, I

remember the look on his face like it was yesterday. A year later my best friend, Kit, put me on the back of his dad's Yamaha and we blasted about four feet into the air off a backyard dirt jump. The mix of thrill and terror as I looked so far down at the ground is frozen in my mind forever.

That same year I watched a pal named Allen ski off a jump at Park City, Utah, and I suppose he sailed 15 feet. I followed him, hitting maybe 10 feet and spraining the hell out of my knee. The cold, quiet moment of my aerial suspension still goes down as one of the most extreme memories of my young life.

My first truly overhead wave at 16 is still vividly clear in my mind, as is the first time I felt the grind of my truck at the top of our neighbor's 10-foot quarterpipe. When I was 20 a crew of college friends and I competed in our first NORBA national mountain bike race. At the end of those 20-plus miles, I don't think any of us had ever felt so exhausted or exhilarated.

Those feelings and memories are extreme too, right?

As I've gotten older, and the extreme is simply everywhere, it has occurred to me that what the "Gods of Extreme" are really pushing here is a feeling we can all relate to. The feeling of Pulling It Off or, if not actually Pulling It Off then, by God, trying and failing in spectacular fashion.

When we go for it, whether on board, bike, or ski, the feeling is extreme. And we go for it because of the rush these sports bring us.

When we can watch the heroes of our extreme sports putting themselves into situations where we hope to be one day, or maybe realize we'll never be in a million years, we can also feel their pleasure—or their pain.

Because we know what it feels like to pull that first air, that first ollie, or that first overhead takeoff. And we *all* know what it feels like to come crashing down to earth.

Though many of the people in this book qualify as famous, most are people just like you and me. They go for it because of the thrill—not because they have to. They go for it whether they get paid or not. They're out there putting their asses on the line for the same rush we all seek.

The rush of the extreme.

—Chris Dixon

Chris Dixon is a Laguna Beach, California, based freelance writer who reports regularly for the New York Times *and is an environmental editor for* Surfer *magazine. He is an avid surfer, snowboarder, and mountain biker, and still bombs around on his downhill skateboard, though after decades of abuse, "My knees sure ain't what they used to be."*

SKATEBOA

RDING

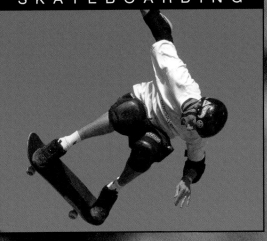

Hell on Wheels

Skateboarding was invented in the early sixties by surfers who called their discovery "sidewalk surfing." Back then they had to make their own skateboards by yanking the wheels off of roller skates and nailing them to the bottom of two-by-fours.

These early, makeshift skateboards were typically ridden barefoot and often out in front of a surf shop by packs of gremmies (sixties surf lingo for young surfers). The style was pure surf with imaginary bottom turns, top turns, pivoting off the tail, cross-stepping to the nose, and driving down the line.

Pedestrians saw a sidewalk, but surfers saw an endless concrete wave. Granted, their boards were hideously crude, but they were too stoked to let their rickety equipment get them down.

Then along came the urethane wheel. Prior to urethane, skateboard wheels were usually made of clay or metal and were very low-performance to say the least. Hit the tiniest pebble on one of those clay-wheeled, two-by-four death sleds, and you were kissing cement pronto. But with urethane came the ability to go faster and stay in control.

Suddenly skateboarding became more than just something to do when the waves were flat. Now you could actually lay down a surf carve at full speed and really lean some body weight into it. All that was missing was the water spraying off your rail.

With this new urethane technology skateboarding began to become more than just a way to mimic the look and feel of riding waves. It became its own unique form of expression. Once weaned from surfing, skateboarding diversified further. Along came the downhill slalom bombers, the twirling flatland freestylers, the renegade backyard pool riders, the vert ramp flyers, and the outlaw street skaters.

Since day one skateboarders have been innovators out of necessity. Before there were skateparks popping up across the country, skateboarders had to go on covert late-night missions to get their ride on. In search of transitioned walls and squared-off planter boxes, skaters continue to frequent corporate business parks after hours in search of skating spots. But these clandestine sessions are typically cut short by Johnny Law. Worst-case scenario during a busted session is a confiscated board. At best you get kicked out with a warning. Game over either way.

But the good news is that illegally riding a planter box in front of the neighborhood credit union isn't essential to having fun. If you're not having fun skating, it's nobody's fault but your own. The only thing limiting a skater is his or her imagination. Just grab your board, walk outside your front door, and go skateboarding. It's that simple (unless you happen to live on a houseboat, that is).

Heck, you don't even technically have to go outside to skate. However skating in the house definitely has its drawbacks, one being the wrath of Mom when she discovers that her tile floor is all scuffed up from your indoor power-sliding session.

A better idea is to just find some concrete, throw your board down, and push off. Voila! Instant fun. And these days there's plenty of concrete around. In fact, the entire world is slowly being paved over one square foot at a time to make room for more Starbucks parking lots. Which is heartbreaking when viewed from an environmental perspective—

but looking on the bright side, at least there'll be that much more terrain to skate.

Never before have there been so many public skateparks in America. And if skateboarding continues its trajectory as one of the fastest-growing sports in the country, it probably won't be long before there's a skate-park in every town across the United States. If not, there's always the new Starbucks parking lot just around the next corner.

—*Gabe Sullivan*

CHRIS GENTRY PERFORMS A JUMP AS BOB BURNQUIST LOOKS ON AT THE SKATEBOARD VERT PRELIMINARY OF THE X GAMES HELD AT THE FIRST UNION CENTER IN PHILADELPHIA ON AUGUST 15, 2002.

Tony Hawk

BORN: CARLSBAD, CALIFORNIA
BIRTH DATE: MAY 12, 1968
HEIGHT: 6'2''
WEIGHT: 170 POUNDS
RESIDENCE: SAN DIEGO, CALIFORNIA
MARITAL STATUS: MARRIED
CHILDREN: 2 SONS

Tony Hawk is the most well-known skateboarder in the world. In fact, his popularity transcends the skateboarding niche. Hawk is the most visible link between the action-sports movement and mainstream audiences. He is—as a typical prime-time sportscaster might dub him— the "King of Extreme."

Hawk first stepped onto a skateboard at nine years old. His older brother Steve is credited for giving Hawk his first board, a blue fiberglass banana board by Bhane. Before Hawk started skating, he was an overachieving spaz case. His die-hard determination was so resolute that at only six years old, striking out in baseball was so devastating that he hid in a ravine until his father pulled him out.

Hawk's escalating frustration concerned his parents enough for them to arrange a psychological evaluation at school. The results revealed that Tony was gifted, and school advisors recommended placing him in advanced classes. The only problem was that his "gift" amounted to having a 12-year-old mind in an 8-year-old body—which explained why young Hawk kept getting so frustrated when his mind was constantly telling his body to do things he wasn't physically capable of. Yet.

Fortunately, thanks to his brother Steve, Hawk's body finally caught up to him when he started skateboarding. Steve noticed that once Tony began to get good at skating it changed his personality. "Finally he was doing something that he was satisfied with," Steve says. "He became a different guy: he was calm, he started to think of other people and became more generous. He was not so worried about losing at other things."

By 12 Hawk was sponsored by Dogtown Skateboards. By 14 he had gone pro, and by age 16 he was the new world champion. Hawk's father Frank drove him up and down the coast of California for skate contests. When Frank grew tired of the existing competitive organization, he founded the California Amateur Skateboard League and the National Skateboard Association. The NSA's high-profile contests were credited with helping the sport surge in popularity during the eighties.

During the next 17 years Hawk entered an estimated 103 pro contests, of which he won 73, and placed second in 19 more. He has the best record by far in skateboarding history. Before retiring from competition in 1999 at age 31, no skateboarder had won even one-third the number of professional competitions as Hawk.

However Hawk's skateboarding career wasn't always as charmed as it may appear on paper. There was a period in 1991 when skateboarding decreased in popularity so severely and so quickly that Hawk thought his career was over. Seemingly overnight his wife Cindy, a manicurist, was suddenly the family provider. Times were so tough that Hawk was scraping by on a daily Taco Bell allowance of $5.

The next few years proved to be a very difficult period for Hawk in both his career and personal life. He sold his four-and-a-half-acre spread in Fallbrook, California (where he built a giant skate ramp on the property and had a smaller ramp wedged between his house and swimming pool). Also gone were the days of buying plane tickets to Hawaii for his friends so everyone could vacation together.

In 1992 Cindy gave birth to their son, Riley. During that time Hawk started his company, Birdhouse Projects, with former Powell pro rider Per Welinder. Two years later Hawk and Cindy divorced. Birdhouse wasn't making money and the young man's future looked bleak.

But Hawk hung in there and continued to develop and perfect his skating skills through the sport's "dead period." The thing that kept him going was his unquenchable passion for skateboarding. "When I'm performing at my best, that's really when I'm most at peace," he says. "This is what I want to be doing, this is what I've been striving for. At the same time it's really exhilarating. My biggest high in

skating is doing something that I've never done before and when I land something for the first time, the rush I get is what I keep coming back for. I think that throughout my whole life I'll be skating at some level, even if it's just for transportation."

The most important thing Hawk has learned from skateboarding is to be self-motivated and persistent. "Growing up I wasn't necessarily the optimum build to be a skateboarder," says Hawk. "I was skinny, I

Clothing, which was then bought by Quiksilver in early 2000. Tony also signed a production/commentating deal with ESPN. And to top it all off, Hawk and Erin had a baby boy named Spencer on March 26, 1999.

Now the proud father of two sons, Hawk would be excited if they someday decided to follow in his skateboarding footsteps, but says he'd encourage them to stay in school too. "I could have got out of school at 16 and made a career as a skater," says Hawk. "But I

"I was skinny, I was small, and not very strong. But if I wanted to learn something, I would never give up; I would just keep trying and trying until I got it."

was small, and not very strong. But if I wanted to learn something, I would never give up; I would just keep trying and trying until I got it. Being that determined has helped me in a lot of aspects of my life."

Hawk's perseverance eventually paid off once skateboarding started to become "cool" again. Things were definitely looking up for Hawk by 1996, when he married his current wife, Erin, and bought a new house in Carlsbad, California. This one didn't have the gigantic ramp, but it did have a new pool with a waterfall, and a trampoline in the yard. Business picked up as well and Birdhouse is now one of the largest skateboarding companies in the world.

Additionally, Tony has signed six-figure endorsement deals with companies like Adio Shoes. And in 1998 he and his family started the kid's skate apparel company Hawk

felt compelled to at least graduate high school. So I'd encourage them to do that and just be well-rounded. If the only goal you have is to be a professional skater, once you reach that goal you might lose your motivation. And there's also a chance that you're going to get hurt and have no more income."

Hawk's worst injury was when he broke his elbow while shooting a commercial. The worst part for him was going through the physical rehab for five weeks; he couldn't straighten his elbow and it was excruciatingly painful.

"When I first started skating again it was a little hard because I knew it was vulnerable," he says. "I could still see the screws under the skin. But after a while I got my confidence back and now I don't even notice it anymore."

While still riding high on the resurging wave of skateboarding's renewed popularity, Hawk decided to retire from competitive skateboarding in 1999. It was no coincidence that he retired on the same day he landed the first ever "900" at the ESPN X Games.

However, for Hawk, retiring doesn't mean he has stopped skating. It just means he's retired from doing contests. In fact Hawk still skates on a daily basis and is still pushing the limits of modern skateboarding. One of the reasons Tony retired when he did was because he finally landed the 900 (two and a half midair spins), something he'd been dreaming about doing for years. The 900 was the last trick on a wish list of tricks he'd written 10 years earlier. The list included the ollie 540, the kickflip 540, the varial 720, and the now legendary 900. It's easy to see why Hawk is pretty happy with the way things have turned out for him—especially considering that in the beginning, he never thought he could make a career out of skateboarding.

Since retiring from competition Hawk's popularity continues to bridge the gap between the action-sports world and mainstream awareness. His award-winning video game, "Tony Hawk's Pro Skater" and "Tony Hawk's Pro Skater 2," are among the most popular video games in the world. In *Cassandra Youth Intelligence Report*'s December 2000 issue, Hawk was rated as one of the four most popular U.S. athletes, along with Michael Jordan, Tiger Woods, and Kobe Bryant. Which explains why when the "Got Milk?" campaign did their "extreme sports" research, they discovered Hawk to be by far the most popular peripheral athlete in the

world. Sporting the requisite milk mustache, Hawk appeared in the ad campaign—upside down and in midflight on his skateboard, of course.

Despite his massive mainstream exposure, Hawk's popularity hasn't waned within the microculture of skateboarding. In fact he continues to be revered as the "Man" at

Birdhouse Projects, is the best-selling skateboard video of all time. His recent instructional DVD and video, *Tony Hawk's Trick Tips Volume 1*, sold over 50,000 copies during its first three weeks on the shelves. At the time of this writing, the Hawk Skateboarding Tour, a televised event in affiliation with ESPN, is in full swing

Hawk's celebrity has helped him create a skateboarding empire. He maintains his own apparel companies, including Hawk Clothing, Hawk Shoes, Birdhouse Skateboards, and an apparel sponsor, Quiksilver.

skateparks worldwide—which explains why it was no big surprise that he was recently voted Skater of the Year by readers of *Transworld Skateboarding* magazine.

A modern-day Midas, everything Hawk touches these days seemingly turns to gold. *The End*, a video produced by Hawk's

motoring its way across the nation.

Hawk's phenomenal skateboarding talent has also taken him to Hollywood, where he's been featured in several movies. He most recently played himself in the comedy *The New Guy*. He's also appeared on numerous television shows and commercials.

Hawk's celebrity has helped him create a skateboarding empire. He maintains his own apparel companies, including Hawk Clothing, Hawk Shoes, and Birdhouse Skateboards, and an apparel sponsor, Quiksilver. His biography, published by Regan Books and titled *Hawk, Occupation: Skateboarder*, sold out of its first printing during prebooking.

But being the "King of Extreme" isn't always easy for His Highness. "I don't think people realize how hectic it gets trying to balance all of this stuff," says Hawk, the skateboarding superhero/husband/father/CEO/-pop-culture icon.

SKATEBOARDING TERMS

AIR

WHAT IT'S CALLED WHEN A SKATER JUMPS OR BECOMES AIRBORNE OFF A RAMP OR OBSTACLE.

ALLEY-OOP

AN AIR TRICK PERFORMED IN THE DIRECTION OPPOSITE THAT WHICH THE SKATER IS MOVING IN.

BACKSIDE

WHEN A TURN OR TRICK IS EXECUTED IN THE DIRECTION THAT THE BACK OF THE BODY IS FACING.

BANK

ANY SLOPED AREA UNDER 90 DEGREES.

BOARDSLIDE/RAILSLIDE

TO SLIDE ON AN OBSTACLE OR LIP WITH THE CONTACT POINT BEING THE UNDERSIDE OF THE BOARD.

CABALLERIAL

WHILE RIDING FAKIE, TO COMPLETE A 360 IN THE AIR AND HEAD BACK DOWN THE RAMP FORWARDS WITHOUT GRABBING. NAMED AFTER STEVE CABALLERO.

CARVE

TO MAKE A LONG, CURVING ARC WHILE SKATING.

DROP IN

TO ENTER THE RAMP OR OBSTACLE FROM THE TOP.

FAKIE

RIDING BACKWARDS.

FRONTSIDE

WHEN A TURN OR TRICK IS EXECUTED IN THE DIRECTION THAT THE FRONT OF THE BODY IS FACING.

GOOFY FOOT

TO RIDE WITH THE RIGHT FOOT FORWARD.

GRIND

TO RIDE ON AN OBJECT LIKE A LEDGE OR HANDRAIL WITH JUST THE TRUCKS MAKING CONTACT.

HALFPIPE

A TYPE OF RAMP THAT IS SHAPED LIKE A "U" AND USED FOR VERT SKATING.

MCTWIST

A 540-DEGREE TURN PERFORMED ON A RAMP. NAMED AFTER MIKE MCGILL.

NOLLIE

MUCH LIKE AN OLLIE, ONLY YOU SPRING OFF OF YOUR NOSE INSTEAD OF YOUR TAIL.

NOSE

THE FRONT OF THE BOARD.

OLLIE

A NO-HANDED AIR PERFORMED BY SIMULTANEOUSLY LIFTING AND PUSHING THE FRONT FOOT FORWARD WHILE TAPPING THE TAIL OF THE BOARD ON THE GROUND OR RAMP SURFACE.

REGULAR FOOT

TO RIDE WITH THE LEFT FOOT FORWARD.

SESSION

A PERIOD OF SKATING.

SWITCH

ANY TRICK WHERE THE TAKE-OFF OR LANDING IS BACKWARDS.

TAIL

THE REAR TIP OF THE BOARD.

SOURCE: EXPN.COM

Bob Burnquist

BORN: RIO DE JANEIRO, BRAZIL
BIRTH DATE: OCTOBER 10, 1976
HEIGHT: 6'2"
WEIGHT: 165 POUNDS
RESIDENCE: RIO DE JANEIRO, BRAZIL
MARITAL STATUS: MARRIED
CHILDREN: 1

Bob Burnquist started skateboarding on the chunky, crackled streets of Brazil when he was 11 years old. Such challenging terrain combined with his lack of exposure to skating trends set the stage for Burnquist's noted creativity.

He appeared on the international skateboarding scene in 1995 at the Slam City Jam in Vancouver, where he turned heads with his innovative style. Burnquist is known for imaginative skating featuring a smooth, switch-stance style. He ended the 2000 season ranked as the number one vert skater in North America and throughout the world, largely because of his incredible ability to do any trick in either regular or switch stance.

Burnquist is also known for not wearing band-aids, even when it's obvious he needs one. "I fell on my head one time at the Rio Sul bowl in Brazil," he says. "I pinched a nerve on my back and couldn't skate for a while. I couldn't wait to skate again, though. I never get discouraged by a slam; if anything, it makes me want to try even harder. If I try something and I don't make it, I'll just get up and try again until I make it— depending on how hard I fall, I most likely will get up and try again. If I can't get up, I'll stay right where I am."

The ever-resilient Burnquist doesn't bother with physical preparation for his contests. "I just get the dates, schedule them in, and fly out," he says. "I always have a few things in mind, though: meet new people, get to know the area, and respect the locals. Contests are just something I do, that if I do good enough, I get some extra money. If not, I had fun and I got to travel. You never lose."

Burnquist's winning attitude apparently carried over into his skating when he won his 2001 X Games gold medal in vert skating. He also took first place in vert at the 1999 Gravity games and was named skater of the year by the readers of *Thrasher* magazine in 1997. In 1998 he was ranked fourth in the world.

Famous for his perpetual smile, Burnquist is enjoying every minute of the pro skating lifestyle. "The Warped tour was fun," he says. "Taking showers and listening to live Bad Religion isn't bad at all."

Like all jobs, though, pro skating isn't always perfect. Turns out the Warped Tour ramp was so small that it really cramped Burnquist's style. "It [the undersized ramp] is very hard on our bodies. Skating every day, two sessions a day, is quite a toll, but I can't complain. I got to travel and have fun."

When not on the road traveling for skate contests, Burnquist likes to street skate in San Francisco. "Street skating downtown at night is always a go," he says. "All the hills are a lot of fun to go down too."

He's also plenty familiar with surfing in the bay area. "The water is very cold," he says. "But the waves are epic and worth the effort."

Burnquist's father is American and his mother is Portuguese. His dad still lives in Rio de Janeiro and his mom and two sisters live in northern California. Burnquist is

fluent in both English and Portuguese and has dual citizenship.

He returns to Brazil four or five times a year and takes the time to invest in the younger skaters there who look up to him as a role model. "It feels great to be such a huge role model for kids," he says. "It's a noble job and a noble experience, but sometimes it gets pretty crazy, so I have to save some time for myself so I don't spread myself too thin."

Skateboarders in Brazil are very strong and self-sufficient. When necessary they can make pretty much everything needed to skate without having to rely on imported equipment. "If for some reason American products couldn't make it down there," says Burnquist, "skaters would still have the products to skate. Maybe not with that much quality, but at least there would be something. The skaters down there have the fire; it's awesome to go back and see all the new faces in skateboarding. Ever since I

moved out, things have been growing and more skaters are roaming the streets and parks of Brazil."

Living in America is a completely different experience from the lifestyle Burnquist was accustomed to in Brazil. "There's a lot of social problems going on in Brazil," he says. "Everywhere you go, all around you see homelessness and you see kids starving. It's just really a completely different world than I live in now. We get to have all these luxuries that I don't necessarily crave, but that are there. And it's great because you can take it. You can give your message as a skateboarder and hopefully people listen to what you have to say. That's the cool thing about it. The only reason I'm excited that [skateboarding] is so mainstream is that we get to reach more people."

And what, you might ask, is this mystical message Burnquist is speaking of? The answer is in his ever-present smile. He is choosing to enjoy life and is inviting us all to get on board.

Andy Macdonald

BORN: BOSTON, MASSACHUSETTS
BIRTH DATE: JULY 31, 1973
HEIGHT: 5'8"
WEIGHT: 165 POUNDS
RESIDENCE: SAN DIEGO, CALIFORNIA
MARITAL STATUS: MARRIED

After graduating from high school in Boston, Massachusetts, in 1992, Andy Macdonald drove to San Diego in a thrashed Datsun with a busted radiator. With only $400 in his wallet, he hit the road in pursuit of his dream of becoming a professional skateboarder.

Little did he know that he'd not only achieve his dream of going pro, but that he'd also become one of skateboarding's most distinguished ambassadors.

These days he frequently finds himself representing skateboarding to general audiences. One such appearance was on *The Tonight Show*, where he chatted up Jay Leno and pulled off a smooth combination of skateboarding tricks in the studio on specially constructed ramps. Other notable mainstream appearances include Macdonald donating "artifacts" such as skateboards, equipment, and photos to put on display at the San Diego Hall of Champions Museum in California and the Australian Gallery of Sport and Olympic Museum, both part of exhibits highlighting action-sports athletes.

The fame resulting from all the exposure occasionally gets a bit comical. One time an overzealous young fan asked Macdonald to spit on his shirt. "I thought it was funny," he recalled. "And no, I didn't spit on the kid's shirt."

In his dealings with the nonskating masses, Macdonald fields frequent questions about the apparent high-risk factor of skateboarding. "We all wear our safety gear," responds Macdonald. "And just like any other sport, there's inherent danger. But just like a hockey player learns how to take a check into the boards, we learn how to fall. It's just a matter of educating people. People see it for the first time and they're like, 'Oh my god, these people are going to kill themselves.' But once you realize the physics and the dynamics behind how we get in the air and how we fall, you realize we do it pretty safely."

Macdonald's worst injury while skateboarding was a broken ankle. Since then numerous rolled ankles have kept him off his board for short periods, but never permanently.

Macdonald first started skating when he was 12. He was playing basketball one day, saw a kid roll across the court on a skateboard, and asked him if he could try it. He and his brother both got boards that Christmas (Macdonald's first board was a Lance Mountain model by Powell), and they started skating together. The first trick Macdonald ever did on a skateboard was a fakie 360 while holding onto a post, which he did on his first try. Then it took him almost a year to learn to ollie up a curb.

But that spirit of perseverance laid a strong foundation for Macdonald's highly successful career in skating. And it's a career he enjoys very much.

What attracts Macdonald to skating is "the freedom and the expression of it," he explains. "There's not any right or wrong way to do it. You just go out and learn through trial and error. It's almost more of an art form than a sport."

Noted for his well-rounded strength in skateboarding, Macdonald is the only skater ever ranked in the world's top 10 in both street and vert styles. His competitive resume boasts six World Cup overall combined titles. He is also credited with seven X Games gold medals and a first place at the 2000 Gravity Games.

Macdonald also won the 1998 *Transworld* Readers' Poll for the Best Overall Skater. Adding to Macdonald's remarkable list of competitive accomplishments is his *Guinness* World Record for the long-distance skateboard jump: 52 feet, 10.5 inches.

Just prior to making his record jump, Macdonald experienced fear like he'd never felt before. "My drop-in was 41 feet high," he says. "It had to be that high to get enough speed to jump so far. That's definitely the most scared I've been . . . but the most fun I've had too."

However such impressive credentials didn't come easy and Macdonald logged some serious time on the road getting to where he is today. His initial cross-country Datsun run was the first of many skate-boarding-related trips that would eventually take him to all but two of the United States (missing only Alaska and South Dakota), to most of Canada and Eastern Europe, and to Africa, Australia, New Zealand, Malaysia, Japan, Brazil, Puerto Rico, Scandinavia, and the Middle East.

One of his scarier trips was when he was in New York during the terrorist attacks on the World Trade Center. Wanting to be with his wife, and knowing that air transportation would be grounded, Andy rented a car and drove across country to his home in San Diego, California, in two and a half days.

EXTREME!

In addition to his phenomenal skateboarding talent and dedication, Macdonald is one heck of a model American—a statement that's especially true now that a U.S. postage stamp is modeled after his image. He has also been invited to the White House, where he gave a speech and introduced then-president of the United States, Bill Clinton, at a press conference for the Partnership for a Drug-Free America committee.

Macdonald prides himself on his efforts to set a positive example for kids. "When I was 12 years old," he says, "I decided not to drink or do drugs. I still don't."

He makes it a point to take time with kids at skate parks and camps not only to teach them how to skate clean but also how to live clean. The simple advice he gives regarding skateboarding is to recognize that it's very hard to do and everyone learns at their own pace. "Don't get caught up in what's cool and what's not," advises Macdonald. "Or with what tricks you should learn. Do whatever makes you happy. Most importantly and above all else, have fun and enjoy it."

Macdonald's dream is that America will someday be filled with public, free-access skateparks. "Right next to basketball courts and tennis courts that nobody is using," he says. "Kids just aren't big on the stick-and-ball sports that their parents did anymore. They'd rather be riding BMX bikes or riding skateboards."

As a role model, Macdonald prefers using a low-key approach by letting his drug- and alcohol-free lifestyle speak for itself—unless, of course, he's giving a speech at the White House.

Bucky Lasek

BORN: BALTIMORE, MARYLAND
BIRTH DATE: DECEMBER 3, 1972
HEIGHT: 5'10''
WEIGHT: 155 POUNDS
RESIDENCE: CARLSBAD, CALIFORNIA
MARITAL STATUS: MARRIED
CHILDREN: 2 DAUGHTERS

Before skateboarding, Bucky Lasek was into riding his BMX bike and break-dancing. Then his bike got stolen and he borrowed a skateboard from a friend. Apparently he liked riding it because after getting a board of his own for Christmas that year, he's barely stepped off since.

These days Lasek is astounded with the popularity and hype surrounding skating. "I'm amazed by it," he says. "I'm seriously amazed by it. I mean, I grew up with Tony Hawk also. As soon as I started skating, four years later I was staying at Tony's house and skating with Tony Hawk, the guy I looked up to forever. And so I was around him and I was around the stages of when he was getting recognized and going places and signing autographs in restaurants and getting free meals. So I was brought up on that. And I was able to take a back seat to it and see it happen."

But then "it" started to happen to Lasek, too. Kids who didn't even skate were approaching Lasek because they recognized him from the video game "Tony Hawk Pro Skater." "I kind of saw it start to happen to me," he says. "And now it's overwhelming. And I'm still in the back seat, kind of just watching it."

In reality, Lasek is definitely not watching from the back seat. Bucky scored the highest vert run ever in the X Games, receiving a score of 98.6 out of 100 possible points in 2000.

As far as the advice he gives to young aspiring skaters hoping "it" will happen to them, he simply recommends having fun and seeing what comes along. He also advises against dropping out of school to go pro. "Don't just drop school because you think you're going to be a professional skater and live off it," he says. "You're going to need school to keep [skating] going."

When Lasek first started learning how to skate he over-rotated on a backside air and fractured his ribs. But that didn't discourage him from investing the next 17 years of his life in skateboarding. Lasek skates an average of three to four hours a day and street skates about every other day when he's not skating vert. "I don't think either street or vert is harder than the other," he says. "It's just hard to be able to do them both well because both require a certain style and approach of execution."

When it comes to vert skating, Lasek has learned to have patience with the unfortunate excess of bad ramp-riding etiquette that's out there. "When you're skating a vert ramp, if someone drops in before you, you don't stay on the ramp," he explained. "You get out, you know? A lot of times people drop in together. And one will drop ahead, and the other will drop behind. The guy who drops behind has to leave. But sometimes when he drops down, you go down. Because when you're skating, there's no line. You know, you put your board down first.

"Now a lot of times there's people who are very competitive. And even though they dropped in behind, they stay on the ramp. And then they don't leave, and they'll do it

again. What I do, I just take my helmet off and just stop. And let them get tired. And then I'll put it back on."

Lasek believes it's important for the progress of skateboarding to always keep trying new things—although it's hard to do that these days with the large amount of competitions and demos he's expected to attend. "All of a sudden the schedule's filling up with premieres and press conferences," he says. "And you're saying, 'OK, where's my time to skate and learn?' So it's very important that you keep skating, and you keep pushing it."

A devoted family man, Lasek juggles his career with his dedication to being there for his wife and kids. A typical day for Lasek involves waking up around 7:00 a.m. to make breakfast for the kids and get Devon, his oldest child, ready for school. Next he'll drop Devon off at school, then run errands with his wife Jen. "Then I'll probably go skate around 2:00," he says, "and get done skating around 6:30, pick up Devon from school, and then I'll come back, probably just relax, eat dinner, and call it a day."

In addition to skating, Lasek stays in shape by surfing and mountain biking.

"When you surf, you work your upper body," he says. "And when you skate, you're just working your legs."

If Lasek wasn't skateboarding, he thinks he'd probably be playing music. He also loves flying, so he says he'd likely wind up pursuing an aviation career. "If I wasn't skateboarding and having the spirit that I have," he says, "I'd probably be doing something pretty similar to it. Something that would be individual, where I would be free to do whatever I wanted to do."

But Lasek is showing no sings of hanging up his board anytime soon. "[Skateboarding] is all I've ever known," he says. "This is what I was raised to do."

Gabe Sullivan is a Laguna Beach, California, based freelance writer whose work has appeared in numerous action-sports publications as well as in Men's Journal *and* Rolling Stone. *He was also a consultant and writer for the animated television show* Rocket Power, *a Nickelodeon series about extreme sports, and his preferred mode of transportation around Laguna Beach is definitely his skateboard.*

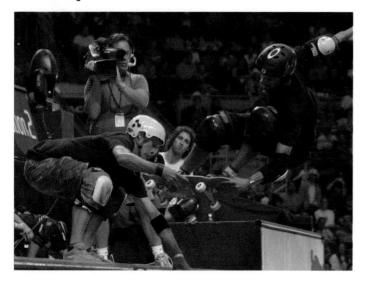

SNOWBOA

RDING

SNOWBOARDING

In the Moment

The father of modern board sports is surfing. Out of surfing sprang skateboarding, which in turn produced snowboarding. Of the three, snowboarding is the only sport adopted by the Olympics—not that Olympic acceptance is a true measure of any given sport's success.

In fact, some Olympic snowboarders, like top-ranked veteran Todd Richards, mentioned the games leaving a "bad taste in my mouth."

The true spirit of snowboarding lives far, far away from the hype of organized competition. Instead, it resides in the hearts of riders willing to climb up a mountain for hours—sometimes even days—just to feel a few moments of bliss while leaning into huge, swooping powder turns and sweeping down steep mountain angles. No contests, no judges, no points system—just freeriding with your friends, adapting to the terrain as it comes. In essence, approaching the entire mountain like one giant wave.

With snowboarding, the actual time spent up and riding lasts infinitely longer than it does while surfing. But the snowboarding trail always ends eventually, and sometimes rather abruptly. Those are the times when your thumping heart suddenly feels like it's beating in your throat as you peer over the ledge of a 50-foot vertical drop to scout your line.

Once committed, time slows down as you accelerate toward the edge. Your ears tingle as your adrenal gland secretes its potent serum into your bloodstream. There is no past. There is no future. Now is all there is.

You take the drop, grab a rail, and spin a 720 by craning your head over your shoulder, causing the rest of your body to follow. Now straightening off, you decompress and brace yourself for the dull thud of impact. You touch down tail-first, recoiling your extended body into your board like a human shock absorber, sucking up the residual momentum not consumed by the five feet of fluffy powder. The natural high you get from cheating death permeates every fiber of your being.

After surviving the big drop, the perma-grin on your face widens even more upon finding that rarest of backcountry treasures: an angled ravine that, by the grace of God, happens to be shaped like a snow-covered skate park. A frozen fun zone, complete with opposing berm-shaped walls transitioning into slightly overhanging lips.

You speed in and carve arcing surf turns, spraying full-sheet, rooster-tail fans of whiteness. . . . Ah, the satisfaction of coming full circle, back to the wave-slashing roots of snowboarding.

Speaking of roots, the first commercially available snowboard, known as the Snurfer, derived its name by combining the words *snow* and *surf*. A guy named Sherman Poppen is credited for inventing the first snowboard in 1965. After seeing his daughter ride downhill standing up sideways on her sled, Poppen attached two skis together for his daughter to "surf" down the snowy incline outside their Michigan home.

His new invention went into production the following year. And the rest, as they say, is history.

In 2000 snowboarding was the fastest-growing sport in America. Which means one thing for sure: surfing's grandchild is all grown up now.

—*Gabe Sullivan*

DANIEL KASS FLIES THROUGH THE AIR ON HIS WAY TO WINNING THE U.S. OPEN HALFPIPE CHAMPIONSHIP ON MARCH 16, 2002, AT STRATTON MOUNTAIN SKI AREA IN STRATTON, VERMONT.

Kevin Jones

BORN: SACRAMENTO, CALIFORNIA
BIRTH DATE: JANUARY 23, 1975
HEIGHT: 5'10"
WEIGHT: 160 POUNDS
RESIDENCE: TRUCKEE, CALIFORNIA
MARITAL STATUS: SINGLE

Prior to becoming a top-ranked snowboarder, Kevin Jones was a die-hard skateboarder who thought snowboarders were a bunch of wussies because the board was attached to their feet. Plus, he didn't approve of their fashion sense in the least. "They wore all that neon," he complained.

But everything changed the night he saw Noah Salaznek and John Cardiel, two skaters he highly respected, snowboarding in the video *Riders of the Storm*. "If Card and Salaz were doing it," says Jones, "I was gonna try it. Cardiel had the sickest steez in that movie! So I tried it [snowboarding] the next weekend and loved it."

Getting into snowboarding proved a good move for Jones, considering he went on to become the most decorated male snowboarder in Winter X Games history, holding nine medals in Big Air and Slopestyle divisions. These results help explain why he was voted the Best Freestyle Rider in the *Transworld nowboarding Magazine* Rider's Poll Awards in 2001.

For having such success in winning contests, you'd think he'd be busy competing all year, but instead Jones only enters an average of three contests per season. Typically he will do the Winter X Games, the Sims World Championships, and one Vans Triple Crown of Snowboarding event.

Rather than spending all his time on the contest circuit, he'd rather be more selective about the events he enters in order to give himself more time to freeride in front of the camera. His real passion is performing in snowboarding action documentary videos.

"I like to film because I liked watching films when I was a tadpole," he says. "I would watch them over and over 'til they wouldn't work anymore; then my mom would get pissed 'cause I ruined all our VCRs."

His favorite is *The Jerk*; he can recite dialogue from the movie on cue: "The Lord loves a working man, never trust Whitey, and if you catch it, see a doctor, and get rid of it."

Jones works consistently with production companies specializing in documenting snowboarding action such as Standard Films, FLF, and Mack Dawg. Shooting on location requires extensive traveling, and life on the road with Jones is a nonstop adventure.

Of a filming trip to France Jones recalls staying in a room "the size of a cereal box" for a month, where his roommate Ardu—apparently feeling too close for comfort—wanted to beat Jones up. Other highlights included 13 feet of new snow and an avalanche that took out a ski lift.

On the same trip fellow snowboarder Jon Sommers broke his back on a road-gap jump. Jones picked up a wound on the trip as well, though his wasn't inflicted while snowboarding. "I got thirteen stitches in my hand from a faulty beverage glass," he says.

Perhaps the injury occurred while having a little too much fun celebrating his birthday in France. "They threw a party for me at the local pub," he says. "They set up a drum kit,

JONES (RIGHT) SHAKES HANDS WITH BEN HINKLEY DURING A SUMMER X GAMES EVENT IN SAN DIEGO.

bass, and guitar; I like to play bass, and we played until the bar closed. That was a cool birthday. Nobody cared that the music sucked."

Initially the French authorities didn't embrace the visiting Americans' habit of jumping over roads on their snowboards. One of Jones' partners-in-crime, Jimmy Halopoff, went to jail for launching a road gap. "The authorities were bummed we didn't involve them," says Jones, "so the next road gap we did, they gave us a bus to jump over, and two dudes with a dump truck came and cut down trees that were in the landing! Twilight zone! Oh, we also had like 20 people helping us build the jump; it took about 12 hours."

The adventure continued in New Zealand, where Jones and his crew had a run-in with a heli-guide who says they were skiing up more powder than they were paying for. "This is after he stopped us on a convex roll on a 32-degree slope to have a 'safety briefing,' " says Jones. "He called us 'stupid Yanks,' and he was from Arizona. Go figure."

But the real low point of the New Zealand trip was when Jones lost his CD case containing 24 of his favorite discs, including six Frank Zappas, four Metallicas, three Primus, one Beethoven, three Rush, two Stevie Ray Vaughns, two Ozzy Osbournes, a Lynyrd Skynyrd, a Willie Nelson, "and last but not least," laments Jones, "my little brother's blues band, RAWB."

When not shaking things up abroad, the drama follows Jones onto the home front. He unwittingly finds himself in the middle of controversies such as the vague origin of a trick called the "chicain." X Games

commentators made the claim that Jones invented the trick and that's when the debate began.

"I think it's funny how people are so worried about the dumbest stuff," says Jones. "I had a guy, I forget his name, come over to my house just to tell me I didn't make that trick up. Apparently his friends in Oregon made it up six years ago, and they called it a 'dump truck.' I still laugh that this guy took time out of his day to make sure I knew I didn't make a trick up, even though I never once said or implied I'd made it up."

Although he doesn't know who invented it, nor does he care, he does think it's a super-fun trick. He also knows that Jimmy Halopoff named it the "chicain" one day in Wolf Creek, Colorado, several years ago and that Andy Hetzel was the first guy he ever saw pull one off.

When the snowboarding scene starts to wear thin, Jones' favorite escape is fly-fishing. Ever sensitive to the fickle whims of fashion, he suffers for his art by wearing fishing waders. "People who don't fish make fun of me," joked Jones. "After I'm done crying I feel a lot better; then I usually need to be held."

Needless to say, Jones is known for his quirky sense of humor. In fact, the only time you'll ever likely see him acting halfway serious is when he's 50 feet in the air spinning over a road gap while looking for a safe place to land. And that's when it becomes evident that Jones is leading the way in proving, perhaps only to himself, that snowboarders are definitely not a bunch of wussies.

ITALY'S GIACOMO KRATTER IN THE U.S. OPEN AT STRATTON IN MARCH 2002.

Terje Haakonsen

BORN: TELEMARK, NORWAY
BIRTH DATE: OCTOBER 11, 1974
HEIGHT: 5'9"
WEIGHT: 165 POUNDS
RESIDENCE: OSLO, NORWAY
MARITAL STATUS: SINGLE
CHILDREN: 1 SON

Norwegian snowboarder Terje Haakonsen is famous for two main reasons. Reason number one: he's the best snowboarder in the world. Reason number two: he boycotted the Olympics.

Prior to snowboarding, Haakonsen had dreams of making it as a professional soccer player. But fate had other plans for the gifted athlete. At the age of 15, Haakonsen placed fifth in the world snowboarding championships. Two years later he was the new world champion.

"That was a fun time," Haakonsen says of that period. "I was the youngest guy on the tour. I was always learning new tricks, figuring out ways to get better."

Haakonsen went on to win two more world titles, five European titles, three U.S. Open titles, and the Legendary Mt. Baker Banked Slalom four times. He has a reputation for being virtually unbeatable in contests.

It remains common knowledge within the ranks of competitive snowboarding that if Terje decides to enter a contest, it typically becomes a contest for second place—behind Haakonsen. He is literally leaps and bounds ahead of the competition.

"He's got phenomenal athleticism and creativity combined with balls," says Jake Burton, founder of Burton Snowboards, one of Haakonsen's sponsors. "And his moves are usually the biggest, usually the most technically difficult, and the cleanest. His influence has been immense. Before Haakonsen, people never dreamed you could go that high."

Which is why, when snowboarding first became an Olympic sport in 1998, it was practically a given that Haakonsen would be getting a gold medal. Virtually all he had to do was show up, blow up, and pick up the gold.

But he decided to skip it because he didn't think certain aspects of the Olympics were good enough for his sport. In fact, nothing about the Olympics seemed to agree with Haakonsen.

Especially annoying to Haakonsen were the bigwig Olympic officials' habit of using chauffeured limousines and staying in fancy hotels while the athletes were being put up in backwoods barracks. Obviously the prospect of such treatment wasn't sitting well with Haakonsen, who at that point was well established as the ultimate snowboarding superstar of the universe.

However, the most unacceptable aspect of Olympic snowboarding for Haakonsen was that skiers were organizing it. "I don't want to do an event if the event is [crappy]," says Haakonsen. "The only reason to do it would be for the good of the sport. But the Olympic Committee put the ski federation in charge of snowboarding. And at the Olympics, the way they did it, the way they made it look, they set the sport back years."

He's talking about the snowboarding event taking place in a heavy rainstorm, with a mandatory two-run routine that restricted innovation and encouraged playing it safe. All this, according to Haakonsen, was the direct result of skiers making the decisions rather than snowboarders.

Instead of going to the Olympics, Haakonsen went to Hawaii, presumably to spend some quality time with his son Matthew. Haakonsen and Matthew's mother, a local Hawaiian, never married, but share in the parenting duties. When not in Hawaii with his mother, Matthew spends several months with Haakonsen in Norway or on the road.

Prior to his son being born Haakonsen fell into a bit of a slump. "Everything around [snowboarding] now is, like, work," said Haakonsen during that time period. "It's too complicated. It's changed the feeling. Before,

my motivation was always to get a lot of different tricks, different terrain. Like my motivation when I was young, not so long ago, was based more on what tricks could I do, how big I could go, how easy I could make it look, the style. But for the last few years my motivation changed. I got more routine, especially in the pipe. I was still trying to go big, but I wasn't trying new tricks. I was, like, not taking chances. I was, you know, stuck."

Although he was seemingly winning at will in virtually every contest he entered during that time, Haakonsen wasn't stretching his limits like he used to. There was little motivating him other than the opportunity to keep collecting the easily

HAAKONSEN IN THE HALFPIPE IN DAVOS, SWITZERLAND.

attainable flow of cash—which is nothing to scoff at when looked at from a strictly business point of view.

And of course the large wad of money earned from being the world's best snowboarder did enable him to buy the luxury loft in Norway and to spend his off-seasons in Brazil, Hawaii, Laguna Beach, California, etc.

But Haakonsen was feeling restless because he knew what he really needed was to get back to pushing, or more accurately, aggressively shoving the

Nearly all parents seem to agree that having children will change your entire outlook on life. It's just one of those things they say you need to experience for yourself in order to fully understand.

Apparently Haakonsen's son Matthew, the little half-Hawaiian, half-Norwegian *menehune*, helped papa Terje get his heart back into flying high once again.

With a renewed passion for snowboarding, Haakonsen went to work planning the Arctic Challenge, an invitational event held on the remote Lofoten

"But for those few years my motivation changed. I got more routine, especially in the pipe. I was still trying to go big, but I wasn't trying new tricks. I was, like, not taking chances. I was, you know, stuck."

perceived performance limits of snowboarding straight through the roof. He needed the satisfaction of doing himself one better. He needed to get back to hucking just a little higher out of the halfpipe. Suspending casually in the air just a little longer. Pulling it all off just a little smoother.

Haakonsen found himself yearning for that old feeling again—the feeling he used to get when he taught himself how to do 360s with his brother on the jump they built in the backyard as kids. But for some reason he wasn't acting on it. He was, as he put it, "You know, stuck."

That is until a *menehune* came along and helped him snap out of it. In Hawaiian, *menehune* means little person, or child.

islands of Norway. Terje and his partners created an event for the riders, by the riders, without the aid of major commercial backing. Invitees enjoyed epic terrain, including a 17-foot-high, meticulously sculpted halfpipe.

According to the select group of rippers at the contest, the overall vibe was epic. Little did this elite group of invited snowboarders know that if it wasn't for a brown-skinned, curly haired boy named Matthew, such a righteous event might never have come together. And who knows, maybe someday little Matthew will be good enough to be an Olympic snowboarder himself—or better yet, make Dad really proud by blowing off the Olympics when they come knocking.

TOMMY CZESCHIN ON HIS WAY TO
WINNING THE MEN'S HALFPIPE
COMPETITION AT WHISTLER, BRITISH
COLUMBIA, ON DECEMBER 7, 2001.

Barrett Christy

BORN: BUFFALO, NEW YORK
BIRTH DATE: FEBRUARY 3, 1971
HEIGHT: 5'2"
WEIGHT: 110 POUNDS
RESIDENCE: VAIL, COLORADO
MARITAL STATUS: SINGLE

After graduating from high school Barrett Christy drove to Lake Tahoe, California, for a vacation and never came back. She decided to stay in Tahoe with the hopes of becoming a better skier.

Skiing, however, wasn't as rewarding as she'd hoped. "I wasn't as good a skier as I thought I was going to be," says Christy. "My legs got all twisted up and I'd lose my poles, and my skis would come off easily."

Frustrated with skiing, it wasn't long before she strapped herself onto a snowboard. "Snowboarding looked easier and more graceful," she recalled. "It wasn't like it came naturally, though. I took a beating. I remember bruising my tailbone the first day. I learned the hard way, without lessons."

Christy lived in Tahoe for two years while teaching herself to snowboard at the Kirkwood ski resort. Eventually losing interest in the Tahoe scene, she moved to Crested Butte, Colorado, where she continued to hone her riding skills. "That's where I think I learned the most about snowboarding," says Barrett. "I had much more time on the snow and made it more of a lifestyle there."

Though she now spends most of her time traveling, Christy keeps a home base in Vail, Colorado, for those increasingly rare gaps in her traveling schedule.

When stopping by the homestead between trips, she tools around town in the Volkswagen GTI she won at the X Games for her overall win in 1999. She's also won a few electric guitars in various contests over the years. She's been, as she puts it, "trying to play" ever since a friend gave her an acoustic in high school.

Christy doesn't seem too worried about not going the Sheryl Crow route on the guitar—although her rock-star status becomes evident the moment she starts busting airs in the halfpipe.

Contributing to the success she's found in snowboarding is her strong ability to stay focused. Not one to look too far ahead, she continually tries to focus her energies on the here and now. "I trust in whatever happens to me," she says. "I just go with it. I'm definitely more in the moment."

Which explains why she didn't start snowboarding with a deliberate career path in mind. But in hindsight she remembers feeling fortunate that she was able to "start snowboarding, make it a priority, and get good at it."

For someone who comes across as spontaneous and in the moment, Christy is a bit of a paradox because she's been known to overanalyze life in general. "A friend of mine once told me I have perplexophrenia," she commented. "That's how she once described me, because I analyze everything. A lot."

It doesn't take much analyzing to figure out that Christy is a world-class snowboarder. She made her debut in the winner's circle in 1994 when she won the Amateur National Halfpipe contest in Vail. Prior to that win she had only competed in a few qualifying events.

Another major breakthrough came in 1997, when Christy became the first and only snowboarder to win both the halfpipe and big-air events at the U.S. Open. From there she went on to the 1998 Olympics in Nagano, Japan, as a member of the first U.S. Olympic Snowboard Team. She finished 14th.

Charging into the next year, she won the 1999 Winter X Games Overall Snowboarding Championship (where she scored her free VW GTI). But much to her chagrin, she sat out part of the 2000/2001 season due to a torn ligament in her left foot. However she did

snowboard for myself," says Christy, "it gets a little grueling." Fortunately she goes on several heli-boarding trips each season and cuts loose in the big-mountain terrain.

Far from a relaxing break from competition, Christy is highly aware of the tremendously different consequences between a wrong move in the pipe and a bad call in the backcountry—consequences that can bury you under tons of avalanching snow in the blink of an eye. "I trust my own judgment," she says, "but I also like to have someone else around to share the second

"I guess I consider myself as a role model. I think anyone who gets any amount of exposure from doing something they love to do ought to consider themselves a role model."

compete at the 2000 X Games, where she took silver in the halfpipe and bronze in the slope style competition.

Other highlights included placing third in the halfpipe at the U.S. Open, second in the Mount Baker banked slalom, and third in the Gravity Games Big-Air division. She was named 2000 Female Rider of the Year by *TransWorld Snowboarding* magazine and made it into the *Guinness Book of World Records* as the holder of more X Games medals than any other athlete. Highlights for 2001 included placing second in the X Games Big Air event and first in the halfpipe at the Grand Prix in Breckenridge, Colorado.

While Christy thrives on the energy of competing, she also likes to go freeriding whenever she can. "If I don't have time to just

and third opinions. I've always got a lump in my throat; it's part of the fun. There's always that aspect of fear, but that's what makes you better."

Equally important to Christy's super-heroine status is her lack of needless fear. And such fearlessness is exactly what it took to launch confident 540s off a huge street kicker at an invitation-only, men-only big-air contest sponsored by Nike in Aspen, Colorado, back in 1996. As the story goes, Christy happened to be in the area so she decided to stop by and make a statement. She boldly sized up the organizers and the kicker, then strapped on her helmet and dropped in with nothing to gain but respect, since she had no chance at winning the $10,000 winner-take-all prize.

Apparently Christy's stunt made an impression on the folks at Nike, who a few years later introduced their new outdoor cross-training shoe: the Air Barrett Christy. "Nike recognized that I do more than just snowboard," she explained. "And there are a lot of people out there like me. I trail-run, hike, and mountain bike. I'm always living out of a suitcase, and I can't pack 20 pairs of shoes everywhere I go, even though I'd like to."

Christy participated in the creative process by working with two designers who took her ideas, wants, and needs, and translated them into a shoe.

In keeping with her hands-on approach with her sponsors, she also helps in the designing of her signature snowboards for Gnu. Most notable are her boards featuring a series of endangered species. On that project she worked with YES (Youth for Environmental Sanity), a grassroots environmental organization that works with kids and focuses on increasing ecological consciousness. YES assisted Barrett in selecting four endangered species needing a boost in public awareness: MacFarlane's four-o'clock (a flowering plant), the ocelot, the California condor, and the American crocodile.

In addition to her genuine desire to give back, Christy also maintains a down-to-earth attitude even though she specializes in flying high. "I guess I think of myself as a role model," responded Christy in a recent interview with EXPN. "I think anyone who gets any amount of exposure from doing something they love to do ought to consider themselves a role model."

If anything, the role model in Barrett Christy should inspire us to live life with more of a passionate, seize-the-day kind of attitude. And if that means extending a vacation to Tahoe into a permanent snowboarding trip, then so be it.

Gabe Sullivan is a Laguna Beach, California, based freelance writer who has contributed regularly to Snowboarder *magazine.*

SNOWBOARDING TERMS

BANKED SLALOM

A SLALOM RACECOURSE WHERE TURNS AROUND GATES ARE SET UP ON SNOW BANKS.

BUST

A TERM FOR LAUNCHING HIGH OFF A JUMP OR HALFPIPE.

FAKIE

A TERM FOR RIDING BACKWARDS.

FREERIDING

SNOWBOARDING ON ALL TYPES OF TERRAIN JUST FOR FUN.

GAP JUMP

A JUMP CONSTRUCTED WITH EMPTY SPACE IN BETWEEN THE TAKEOFF AND THE LANDING. NOT CLEARING THE GAP USUALLY HAS DETRIMENTAL CONSEQUENCES.

GRAB

TO GRAB EITHER EDGE OF THE SNOWBOARD WITH ONE OR BOTH HANDS WHILE AIRBORNE.

HAAKON FLIP

AN INVERTED SWITCH 720. A HALFPIPE TRICK IN WHICH THE RIDER APPROACHES THE BACKSIDE WALL RIDING FAKIE AND ROTATES IN THE BACKSIDE DIRECTION WHILE GOING UPSIDE DOWN. INVENTED BY TERJE HAAKONSEN.

HALFPIPE

A SNOW STRUCTURE BUILT FOR FREESTYLE SNOWBOARDING. IT CONSISTS OF OPPOSING RADIAL TRANSITION WALLS OF THE SAME HEIGHT AND SIZE. SNOWBOARDERS UTILIZE THE HALFPIPE TO CATCH AIR AND PERFORM TRICKS BY TRAVELING BACK AND FORTH FROM WALL TO WALL WHILE MOVING DOWN THE FALL LINE.

900 AIR (ALSO KNOWN AS NINE)

THE SNOWBOARDER ROTATES 900 DEGREES IN THE AIR AND LANDS RIDING FAKIE. IN THE HALFPIPE THE RIDER APPROACHES THE WALL RIDING FORWARD, ROTATES 900 DEGREES, AND LANDS RIDING FORWARD.

OLLIE

A METHOD TO OBTAIN AIR WITHOUT A JUMP BY FIRST LIFTING THE FRONT FOOT, THEN LIFTING THE REAR FOOT AS YOU SPRING OFF OF THE TAIL.

SLOPESTYLE COMPETITION

A FREESTYLE EVENT IN WHICH THE COMPETITOR RIDES OVER A SERIES OF VARIOUS KINDS OF JUMPS. HE OR SHE IS THEN JUDGED ON THE PERFORMANCE OF TRICKS AND MANEUVERS.

SWITCHSTANCE (SWITCH)

THE TERM FOR PERFORMING A TRICK WHILE RIDING FAKIE.

TABLE TOP

A JUMP IN WHICH THE TAKEOFF AND LANDING ARE CONNECTED BY A LONG, FLAT SURFACE. IDEALLY ONE WANTS TO CLEAR THE "TABLE" AND LAND ON THE DOWN SLOPE.

360 AIR (ALSO KNOWN AS THREE)

THE SNOWBOARDER ROTATES 360 DEGREES IN THE AIR AND LANDS RIDING FORWARD. IN THE HALFPIPE, THE RIDER APPROACHES THE WALL RIDING FORWARD, ROTATES 360 DEGREES, AND LANDS RIDING FAKIE.

TRANSITION (TRANNY)

THE RADIAL CURVED SECTION OF A HALFPIPE WALL BETWEEN THE FLAT BOTTOM AND THE VERTICAL. A SNOWBOARDER PUMPS AND RIDES THE TRANSITION TO GAIN SPEED, TO CATCH AIR, AND TO LAND.

VERTICAL (VERT)

THE VERTICAL TOP PORTION OF A WALL IN A HALFPIPE.

SOURCE: EXPN.COM

BMX

Flying High

Freestyle BMX isn't for wussies. It never has been. When it started back in the seventies, skateboarding and motocross were the reigning alternative sports, and BMX freestyle was the underdog's underdog.

At that time it had no name—just a few riders who liked to do tricks on their 20-inchers. One of them was Bob Haro.

A skateboarder who was excited by the possibilities of BMX bikes, Haro was one of the first BMXers who edged his way into skateparks, dropped into drained swimming pools alongside boarders, and quietly sparked a never-before-seen style of bike sport.

These BMX visionaries hardly got a warm welcome in the skateparks or pools they rode—a hallmark of the sport that, sadly, still exists today. But as their tricks became more advanced they harnessed some well-deserved respect and, by the early eighties, "trick riding" had gained some legitimacy. It also got an official name—freestyling—courtesy of the 1984 launch of *Freestylin'* magazine.

Spawned by the editors at *BMX Action* magazine and dedicated solely to the art of bicycle stunts and the freewheeling lifestyle its young masters represented, *Freestylin'* sparked a fervor for bike stunts that had kids around the nation accelerating up and down homemade ramps, attacking dirt jumps, and envisioning a future filled with fame and fortune. The American Freestyle Association (AFA) entered the picture that same year.

Without a doubt, the sky was the limit.

Or was it? By the late eighties, like all things that go up, freestyle's popularity had again plummeted down. Some say it was a victim of its own overblown hype; others say the bikes weren't improving at the same rate as the riders. Whatever doomed freestyle BMX in the late eighties, the fact remained: it was dying a painful death.

By 1990 the AFA had shut its doors, major BMX freestyle bike manufacturers had pared down or bowed out of the industry, and once again, freestyle BMX was the underdog. The persistent few who knew the sport's, and their own, potential refused to hang up their Vans; they kept the passion for their sport chugging via homemade videos, local jams, and their own skilled progress. All they needed was a leader to bring them back together again.

Enter Mat Hoffman, a freestyle showstopper who was, without question, the sport's last hope. In the industry, as on the ramp, Hoffman was a revolutionary who revised people's opinions of freestyle's potential.

He raised the bar on stunts in the late eighties, and in the early nineties on more stunts, bike design, and competition possibilities. As his success in the industry solidified, other rider-run companies cropped up, hoping to meet the demands of a ballooning population of riders and helping to fuel the rebirth of freestyle.

The revolution picked up steam as kids around the world found their calling. It wasn't long before heavy-hitting sports authorities like ESPN sat up and paid attention. In 1995, freestyle BMX charged out of the underground to shine on a major stage at ESPN's first X Games. Since then, the coverage and the tricks have only gotten bigger.

Today kids can jam and/or compete in four different BMX freestyle disciplines. In dirt jumping, the name of the game is mad speed and big air. Riders launch from dirt or metal ramps, shoot over obstacles like cars, and execute wild moves in midair. Vert, or half-pipe, demands that riders speed up the vertical walls of a U-shaped structure and, like dirt jumpers, pull huge moves while soaring above the pipe.

Flatlanders are all about finesse and balance. They operate on a flat slab of concrete, hence the name, gelling their bike and body in a series of complicated moves that some people consider a kind of supersmooth bike dancing. Street riders take on whatever they roll up to while riding. Usually executed on built-to-spec rails, ramps, and gaps for competition, day-to-day street riding requires that a rider be prepared to grind, jump, and launch off whatever opportunity his or her cityscape offers.

Want to know more? Read on and learn from the best . . .

—*Lynda Twardowski*

Dave Mirra

BORN: SYRACUSE, NEW YORK
BIRTH DATE: APRIL 4, 1974
HEIGHT: 5'9"
WEIGHT: 155 POUNDS
RESIDENCE: GREENVILLE, NORTH CAROLINA
MARITAL STATUS: SINGLE

They call him Miracle Boy. It's a nickname that is usually assigned to kids born in test tubes, or people rescued from mountaintops or ocean-tossed inner tubes—not a guy who rides a bike.

But then again, Dave Mirra doesn't ride a bike; he flips, flies, spins, and slams on a bike. He is, arguably, the best BMX freestyler.

The most decorated athlete in alternative sports, Mirra has taken home 13 gold medals and three silvers from ESPN's X Games, was voted *BMX Magazine*'s Freestyler of the Year in 1999, BMX Rider of the Year at the 2001 Action Sports and Music Awards, and *Transworld BMX* magazine's number one Ramp Rider in 2002.

By all accounts, his is one of the most recognizable faces and names in alternative sports, thanks to mad media exposure that has plastered his mug everywhere from the cover of *Sports Illustrated for Kids* to the pages of *Rolling Stone* and *ESPN Magazine*. Mirra has also appeared on *The Late Show with David Letterman* and *Good Morning America*.

Add to that the goodies to which he's lent his name and image—Dave Mirra action figures, finger bikes, bubble gum, trading cards, video games, knee guards, signature shoes with DC shoes, signature bikes with Haro, and several pairs of signature shoes for

former sponsor Adidas—and it's safe to say Mirra has had quite a hand in elevating the world of alternative sports into the mainstream, a miracle in and of itself.

So where did his meteoric rise to the top begin? Well, not in a test tube. Mirra was born the old-fashioned way on April 4, 1974, to Mike and Linda Mirra in Syracuse, New York. He was only four years old when he first learned to ride a bike.

At that time the Schwinn Bicycle Company's Sting Ray was transforming the face of bicycling in America. It was the first popular BMX bike, notable for its rugged, dirt-grabbing tires and potential for speed, and American kids loved it. Other BMX bikes followed and soon homemade ramps and dirt trails started springing up all over the country.

Mirra was one of the kids who couldn't resist the thrills this new breed of bike offered. Along with his brother Tim and friend Sean Wagner, Mirra would ride all day, every single day. The threesome worked to learn and then perfect early moves, like the 180 bunnyhops and curb jumps Sean's older brother and his friends were pulling off. By the time he was five years old, Mirra was on the ramp.

He was young, and his natural talent and fire for BMX were undeniable. But like any kid, he had some kinks to work out. The difference? Mirra was willing to work and work and work until he did. He started attempting tricks at 10 years old, entering competitions, sponsored by Haro, at age 13, and nailing 360s on wooden ramps at age 15. By then it was obvious that his workhorse mentality was paying off. While still a high schooler, Mirra went pro.

He'd probably tell you himself: It wasn't that he had his eyes on any pro prize or a hankering for fame and fortune. He just wanted to ride as well as he could, and he was willing to do what needed to be done in order to accomplish that. He once said, "I gave up a lot of my life for my bike riding, but it's been worth it. I've been injured and I've gotten up and kept riding."

It's that determination that has made Mirra's mental prowess on the ramp as stunning as his physical feats. He says he

results. For Mirra, the 720 (spinning with two complete rotations) was the trick that, for a long time, seemed out of his reach. "I either do an awesome one or I wreck it. It plays with my mind," he said.

No doubt he kept plugging away at that one, just like he did to conquer his favorites: the no-handed 540, flairs, and one-handed tailwhips. As much as Mirra likes to swing those moves, though, it's the public's favorite—the double backflip—that confirmed Mirra's notoriety as a miracle boy.

He was young, and his natural talent and fire for BMX were undeniable. But like any kid, he had some kinks to work out. The difference? Mirra was willing to work and work and work until he did.

visualizes a lot, working as hard to understand a trick in his mind as he does executing it in midair. Visualization and practice, he says, are the ways to execute a move well.

In an online chat on EXPN.com, Mirra told a fan that mental prepping is the key to success in competition. "You have to feel confident in how you are riding; the mental part is everything. It's just being dialed at the time and creating peace for yourself. You don't worry about the little things."

As with his mental efforts, Mirra's physical toil is nonstop. He likes to supplement his mind's-eye vision of the trick he wants to accomplish with steady practice on the ramp, working his tricks back to back, over and over, until he is completely happy with the

On May 7, 2000, during the qualifying runs at Utopia in Raleigh, North Carolina, Mirra made history by executing a perfect double-flip, a trick no rider had ever before managed in competition. Two of the judges gave Mirra perfect 100s. Soon after, Mirra said he hoped to see jumps in parks as big as the one in Utopia (the box was 6-feet tall, 14-feet long, and the vertical wall topped out at 20 feet) so he could keep springing those double-flips.

Sound kind of fearless? Well, Mirra is a stud, there's no doubt about that, but he'll readily admit he's still human—and he has the bumps and breaks to prove it. He's had his spleen removed, his shoulder broken, and by some really strange bit of bad luck, has been hit by drunk drivers, twice.

The first time it happened was in 1991. Mirra was at the wheel of the rig that shuttled him and other riders from city to city during a GT tour, and all was going well until an intoxicated driver racing behind him rear-ended the rig. Although Mirra and his crew weren't badly hurt, the drunk driver's face got up close and personal with his own windshield.

The second time it happened, Mirra was simply walking across a street when a drunk driver plowed on through. This time around it was Mirra who kissed the windshield. He was also tossed up and over the car about 20 feet by his own estimate.

In September 2001 Mirra took a spill during a normal slide out on the vert ramp a week before the Gravity Games and was forced to sit the games out so his knee would have time to heal. Recently, at the 2002 Vans Triple Crown in Charlotte, it was a simple cut to the elbow that sent Mirra to the hospital. Word is, the stitches got infected and Mirra had to endure surgery so doctors could remove some fluid.

For good reason he admits that certain stunts scare him (although, he says, it depends on the day) and that he doesn't dare tackle the ramp without his protective gear: full-face helmet, elbow pads, kneepads, and gloves. Still, the fear of pain falls far short of the power of Mirra's love of the sport and the challenge of the competition.

The competition is made up of some of his best friends. In Greenville, North Carolina, the small town Miracle Boy made his home when he was just 21, he rolls deep with a crew of BMX greats like Mike Laird, Ryan Nyquist, Colin McKay, and lots of other up-and-comers. The Greenville bunch constantly push each other to imagine, attempt, and nail bigger and better moves.

Mirra says he is also inspired by the competitors who don't live so close by, as well as by the guys who came before him. He counts Brian Blyther, Ron Wilkerson, Dennis McCoy, Bob Haro, Pete Augustin, and Mat Hoffman among his biggest inspirations.

Don't be surprised if you hear Mirra adding Tiger Woods' name to his list of influences. Believe it or not, the calm, slow-paced game of golf is one of the extreme rider's favorite sports. He often jokes that when he's too old to ride his bike, fans will be able to find him walking the fairways of the PGA Tour.

In the meantime he is happy to hit stick for fun and for good causes like The Dream Factory, an organization which works to grant dreams to critically or chronically ill children between the ages of 3 and 18 years old, and for which Mirra has hosted "X-treme Fun for X-treme Causes," a three-day, dinner/ridefest/-golf outing/fundraiser.

Yep, he's faster than a speeding bullet, he leaps tall verts with a flawless jump, and in between countless competitions and tours like Tony Hawk's Boom Boom Huckjam Tour, his own Dave Mirra BMX Super Tour, and dozens of others, he still finds time to make the wishes of little kids come true. Does this guy ever take a day off? Well, it's rare, but when he does, he admits he's still working hard, planting scads of trees around his house in Greenville, scouting for that perfect pool table to put inside his digs, or thinking about that next trick.

Fans hope that last one will keep him busy—and coming back to the ramp—for years to come. By all indications, that's Mirra's hope too. As he told Scot McElwaney, editor of BMXonline.com, in 2001, "I think I'm still warming up. I'm going for another five or six years at least. I don't really have a date to put on it to be honest. I feel healthy. I'm still having fun riding, so I really can't put a number on it. It would be unfair to say five or six years because I think I'm still going to be around as long as I'm having fun, still riding, and still healthy. I don't have any idea [how long], but a long time."

Mat Hoffman

BORN: OKLAHOMA CITY, OKLAHOMA
BIRTH DATE: JANUARY 9, 1972
HEIGHT: 6'
WEIGHT: 160 POUNDS
RESIDENCE: OKLAHOMA CITY, OKLAHOMA
MARITAL STATUS: MARRIED
CHILDREN: 1 DAUGHTER

In 1982 Mat Hoffman was 10 years old, and he had an idea. He wanted to build a ramp so he could do tricks on his BMX bike. He would slink up to TG&Y, a local discount store by his house in Edmond, Oklahoma, and sneak peeks at the few BMX magazines on the racks. He'd peer at the ramps, check out the tricks, and hopefully get a good idea of how both were built before a clerk came along and shooed him home.

Obviously, his scoping methods were quicker than the clerks trying to keep up with him. With the help of his uncle, Hoffman managed to build a ramp of his very own and imitate those tricks he saw in the magazines. Soon Hoffman's skills were surpassing the tricks available to be copied.

Never one to idle around waiting for change, Hoffman, in what has become his signature style, decided to take action and become the instrument of change himself. He busted his hump—not to mention a few bones—to invent bigger, sicker, wilder tricks.

The results of his efforts? Besides a friendly familiarity with various emergency-room personnel, his results include the flair, the fakie flip (or backflip fakie), the 900, the no-handed 540, and more than 50 other original tricks. With these and a litany of signature style variations, Hoffman forever changed the face of bicycle stunts and, in doing so, made himself a major pioneer in the freestyle movement. Not bad for a kid with a homemade ramp, eh?

Although his master moves weren't all made by the time he hit it big at the amateur competitor level in 1982, his talent and creativity on a bike were obvious right away. It didn't take long before another bicycle pioneer, Bob Haro—the famed skateboarder-turned-BMX-rider who basically invented bicycle freestyle in the seventies—and Haro's brother, Ron "Rhino" Haro, recognized Hoffman's promise.

The Haro brothers tagged Hoffman as a revolution waiting to happen and began sending him out on tours in the United States and, soon, around the world. At about this time Hoffman was dubbed the "Condor." It was for good reason. Hoffman's popularity soared in sync with his tricks, and together Hoffman and the innovative art of BMX freestyle rocketed to levels never seen—let alone attempted—ever before.

In 1992 he built a 21-foot vert quarterpipe, the tallest the world had seen at that point, and then dropped in and launched himself 20 feet into the air, setting the first high-air world record. In 1993 he launched from a 40-foot roll with the boost of a small motor and caught 20 feet of air again, but slammed down and ruptured his spleen.

No matter. By 1994 he was at it again. This time sans engine, but again on a 21-foot-tall quarterpipe, he outdid his own record and tacked on three more feet of air.

It still wasn't enough for Hoffman. By 2001 he was looking to best his own record once more, this time in a vert quarter pipe that

topped off at 24 feet. Hoffman dropped in and hit 26.5 feet above the coping, a height no rider or skateboarder had, as of yet, even come close to. (That same year Mirra did come close, however, hitting 19 feet on an 18 1/2-foot vert halfpipe.)

Is there any height Hoffman won't go to with his bike? Well, considering he also trekked to Norway to go base jumping with his bike from cliffs 3,500 feet high, the answer is no, probably not.

sponsored, "You don't need sponsors to make it as far as I have. All you need is a bike and a will to keep challenging yourself with it."

Once he was on his own Hoffman did just that. As he catapulted to the top of the stunt competitions, Hoffman rode his success in the business arena too, creating Hoffman Promotions in 1991. One of Hoffman Promotions' first orders of business was to recruit the best riders Hoffman knew. His plan? To create a show team that would tour

The talent and tricks Hoffman was pulling proved to be more than the bikes at that time could handle. Unwilling to complain about weak frames, Hoffman hit the drawing board and designed his own bike.

Fact is, the man is fearless. And 20 years, countless injuries, and 14 surgeries after taking his first trick, we're still waiting to see what he'll do next.

And for good reason. As impressive and revolutionary as every one of his stunts has been, they aren't the only reason Hoffman is a legend to which the likes of phenoms like Mirra pay huge respects. Hoffman is a hero in the freestyle world because every time he soars to new heights, he takes the freestyle community with him.

When he was only 19 years old he had a vision for the future of BMX freestyle and was determined to raise the bar for a pro's potential. To do that Hoffman knew he'd have to take the reins of his own career and part ways with his primary sponsor. As he once told a fan who asked him how to get

the country, promoting and expanding the sport and helping it to gain the respect and legitimacy it deserved. The Sprocket Jockey Bicycle Stunt Team was born.

Unfortunately, the talent and tricks Hoffman and his team were pulling proved to be more than the bikes at that time could handle. Unwilling to complain about weak frames when he thought he could do something about them, Hoffman hit the drawing board and designed his own bike. The result was a stunning BMX that could do exactly what its riders did every day: take a killer pounding and keep coming back for more. Hoffman Bikes was born.

With both a promotional company and a bike company under his belt, Hoffman was ready to take freestyle even further. He established a major competition, the Bicycle

Stunt Series (commonly referred to now as the BS Series), which teamed up with ESPN for some major televised airplay in 1995. Today it's one of the most respected events for freestylers.

Never one to leave the up and comers without a venue in which to compete, Hoffman later created the Crazy Freakin' Bikers Series (CFB), which serves as a prelude to the next level of competition, the BS Series. Born from all of the above is the Hoffman Sports Association, which organizes the X Games and all bicycle-related stunt events.

You'd think all this business would switch Hoffman's focus from BMX freestyling to "Hoffman Incorporated," but he told EXPN.com that nothing could be further from the truth. "I really don't see it as a corporation; it's just my life. I ride bikes, make bikes, put contests and other bike events on, and make some TV shows because those are the things I am into. . . . I just wanted to have control over my own destiny and do things the way I envisioned them without ever having to compromise or conform to anything."

Spoken like a true innovator. A leader in the industry and on the street, Hoffman has said time and time again that it doesn't matter to him what the competition is doing during a contest. While he will drop in with one or two tricks in his head, he says he likes to let the run shape itself so he can go with what he feels at that moment. No routine, no choreographed bit—just him, his bike, and a whole lot of potential.

Potential is what Hoffman believes BMX is all about, and aside from his own personal successes, he's made it his mission to make the rest of the world see that too. As such, he's made it a priority to stay in close touch with his fans via frequent Q&A sessions and a journal he keeps online. In the latter, Hoffman works to inspire other young BMXers to control their own destiny and push to get the public— namely, public skateparks that ban bikes and local governments—to accept and even relish the potential riding offers kids.

He doesn't stop there. He has publicly denounced big companies like the shoe manufacturer Vans, whose skateparks have been known to limit bike sessions and favor board (and, ironically, even inline) sessions. In his online journal in October 2000, Hoffman ranted, "As for Vans, I don't get it! They let inliners in, and they don't even *wear* shoes. A little support for an industry you make money off of would be nice."

True to form, Hoffman's concern and support has always been aimed at the ones who make the sport what it is: the riders. He rallies fans and fellow bikers to challenge other people's opinions about their sport, to promote it, and to learn from each other.

He does his part to help too. In 2000 he asked riders to send their best local zines (homemade magazines) dedicated to riding to Hoffman Bikes. In turn, Hoffman promised to run reviews and subscription info for the best zines in Hoffman Bikes' official zine so everyone could keep up on the scene nationwide.

Indeed, Hoffman is a man on a mission. Although he's now 30 years old and a devoted new dad, Hoffman shows no sign of stopping—only adapting. One example? Last summer on the Tony Hawk tour, he followed the tour bus in the Hoffman family wagon so he could take his baby girl with him.

If that sounds a little slow, don't panic. Hoffman never sticks to speed limits for long. That summer he and fellow family man Hawk left their kids behind to slip into a Ferrari and race down Germany's Autobahn at 180 miles per hour. Does this mean a new career is in the works? Put it this way, says Hoffman: "I know what I'm getting into when I go through my midlife crisis."

BMX TERMS

AIR

IF BOTH WHEELS LEAVE THE SURFACE OF THE EARTH YOU'VE GOT IT.

CARVE

THE CURVED LINE A RIDER FOLLOWS ALONG ANY SLOPED AREA.

COPING

THE LIP ALONG THE TOP OF A RAMP OR PIPE.

DIALED IN

WHERE YOU'RE AT WHEN YOU'RE IN "THE ZONE," OR ONE WITH THE TASK AT HAND.

DROP IN

ROLLING INTO THE RAMP, OR PIPE, FROM ABOVE.

FAKIE

TO RIDE UP A RAMP, CATCH AIR, LAND FACING THE SAME DIRECTION, AND THEN ROLL BACK DOWN THE RAMP BACKWARDS.

GRIND

TO SLIDE ALONG THE RIDGE OF AN OBSTACLE, SUCH AS A HANDRAIL OR CURB, OR THE COPING ON A RAMP USING YOUR WHEEL PEGS.

HALFPIPE

USED IN VERT, A RAMP THAT IS SHAPED LIKE A "U" SO THAT ITS SIDES ARE AT A 90-DEGREE ANGLE.

HIP

THE POINT WHERE TWO RAMPS COME TOGETHER—USUALLY AT A 45-DEGREE ANGLE.

ONE-FOOTER

A BASIC TRICK THAT ENTAILS KICKING ONE FOOT OUT TO THE SIDE WHILE IN MIDAIR— GATEWAY TO NO FOOTERS, CAN CAN, ETC.

SESSION

THE NAME GIVEN TO THE TIME DURING WHICH RIDERS PRACTICE AND RIDE TOGETHER.

TRANSITION

THE CURVED PART OF ANY TERRAIN THAT IS AT AN ANGLE EQUAL TO OR LESS THAN 90 DEGREES.

VERT

OTHERWISE KNOWN AS VERTICAL, VERT IS THE NAME GIVEN TO A RAMP OR WALL THAT SITS AT A 90-DEGREE ANGLE.

X-UP

A TRICK IN WHICH THE RIDER, IN MIDAIR, TWISTS HIS HANDLEBARS 180 DEGREES SO THAT HIS ARMS FORM AN "X."

SOURCE: EXPN.COM

Dennis McCoy

BORN: KANSAS CITY, MISSOURI
BIRTH DATE: DECEMBER 29, 1966
HEIGHT: 5'8"
WEIGHT: 150 POUNDS
RESIDENCE: KANSAS CITY, MISSOURI
MARITAL STATUS: MARRIED

Tennis "DMC" McCoy is renowned for one thing in BMX freestyle: everything. The only rider to hold titles in street, dirt, vert, and flatland riding, he is the try-all, do-all, conquer-all phenom of BMX freestyle.

From the day he entered the pro scene in 1986, McCoy has dominated, seizing the top Overall ranking year after year . . . after year . . . after year--well, you get the picture. He snagged his last one in 1995. What happened in '96? It had nothing to do with McCoy's performances; the Overall category was actually eliminated.

No matter for McCoy. He went on to be named the King of Concrete with a number one ranking in the street division that year. In the years following, he turned his attentions to the then-new ESPN X Game competitions and so far has nabbed five X Games medals in street *and* vert.

His flexibility—some call it elasticity—in switching between the freestyle disciplines translates to pure passion for riding. Time and again he tells other up-and-coming riders to put their efforts into riding everything and anything instead of condemning one aspect of freestyle as less than another. In the long run, he says, maintaining a field of options in the freestyle arena is what has helped to keep him from

burning out and has perpetuated his passion for the sport all these years.

Make no mistake: it's been a lot of years. McCoy, born December 29, 1966, estimates that he's been on a bike since he was about four years old. As he tells it, his mom hoisted him atop the seat, gave him a shove, and he was off peddling . . . directly into a bush.

For McCoy that first crash was more fun than his first ride, and with that fear of falling out of the way, he held nothing back. Soon he was jumping curbs, popping wheelies, and tearing up the neighborhood. By the eighties, it was clear bikes were McCoy's life.

He started entering races and eventually turned his attentions to freestyle, in all its forms. In 1986 he went pro, kicking off 10 years of back-to-back top Overall rankings and what would come to be known as McCoy's "Decade of Domination."

His merciless domination in the sport has earned him more than medals (and, OK, a lot of well-deserved respect from the entire free-style community). McCoy is also noteworthy for the scores of corporate sponsorships he's had throughout the years. In a sport where sponsorship is the Holy Grail, and often the only hope a rider has of fulfilling his dreams, McCoy's lion's share would seem to put him at risk for some nasty backbiting and jealous slams from his fellow riders.

Not so. That's just another part of what makes McCoy's career so remarkable. Unlike many fixtures in the sport, McCoy's name is rarely brought up with anything less than reverence.

Scores of reporters have noted that he's managed to escape being a trash-talk topic and given their own reasons why, but

BMXtrix.com finally got McCoy to give his opinion on the feat. "I don't know, man," he says. "Maybe they just feel sorry for me cause I'm the older guy and they just leave me alone. Maybe it is because I have been around forever. I saw the sport through its glam phase. I didn't get caught up in the whole phase of buying Porsches. I didn't quit when the money fell out of the sport. I stayed into it. So maybe that's got something to do with it. Or maybe it's just because I'm such a big sh-- talker that nobody wants to talk crap about me because they are afraid of what will come back."

injury list through the years, it's clear that award is actually right on target. Perhaps it's because he's been riding longer than just about anybody competing nowadays, but without a doubt, McCoy wields a resume of pain the likes of which few riders can compete with.

Besides the usual, numerous concussions, broken bones, dislocated parts, and assorted major and minor surgeries, McCoy has endured a collapsed lung and a slam on a ramp during the BS 2000, which hit him so hard that one of his shoulders permanently sits an inch lower than the other. In his

"My favorite type of riding really is just going out street riding with my friends, just because it's so laid back. You can just screw around or go for burly stuff or get chased by people or whatever."

Don't be fooled: McCoy always has been less interested in talk than he has been in action. Just ask Rick Thorne, who lost his bike to the Atlantic Ocean in the dead of winter when McCoy took—and won—a $20 bet with Mat Hoffman. His penchant for practical jokes aside, Hoffman is a well-regarded good guy. He works hard, thanks his wife for her support in every interview, and never fails to mention the sponsors who helped get him where he's at—even if, like Mongoose, whom he left in 1997 for K2, he's not signed with them any longer.

Hardly what you'd expect from the guy who was awarded the 2001 "Tough as Nails" award, eh? Of course, if you've followed his

opinion, damage like that is pretty minor. His worst injury, he says, was a wrist injury he sustained in 1996. For 14 weeks he couldn't even tie his shoe.

Now 36 years old, McCoy seems to have the same view on injuries that he had when he was a toddler careening off into the bushes: pain is a small price to pay for the fun that's to be had on a bike. No doubt that's why he's still laughing about a comment he once made to a reporter when he was 20 years old--that he hoped to ride competitively until he was 30 years old.

At that time, he says, people laughed at him. The sport was a young kid's sport and no one believed anyone that "old" could withstand the beatings freestyle routinely handed out. No doubt those naysayers are eating their words as they watch him shred in competitions today.

Chances are, they'll keep eating for a while. Although McCoy hasn't made any major announcements concerning his future plans, retirement doesn't appear to be an option anytime soon. He competed in both the X Games and Gravity Games in 2002, as well as shows galore. In the summer of 2002 he joined Dave Mirra, Hoffman, Kevin Robinson, and John Parker in Tony Hawk's Boom Boom Huckjam touring show to shred up and down a portable ramp system made of custom-built steel and European birch, rumored to cost more than $1 million. No doubt it was worth the ride.

Fame, fortune, mad tours, and major competitions may keep him coming back for a while, but if you had to pinpoint what it is that keeps him riding, McCoy's answer has always been the same: riding. He often says that he tries to keep the touring to a minimum and the contests to just the larger ones just so he can stay home and spend as much time as possible just riding for fun. Besides the huge vert ramps he spends weeks building, he likes to tear up the town with the locals he rides with at home in Kansas City.

What form of freestyle does he tend to lean toward when he's on his own time? "My favorite type of riding really is just going out street riding with my friends, just because it's so laid back," he tells BMXtrix.com. "You can just screw around or go for burly stuff or get chased by people or whatever. But I love a good skatepark session too. It's always a blast where there's a good park with a vert ramp and a street course and mini ramps and tons of stuff where you can play all night with the music cranking."

His favorite music to jam to is everything from The Beatles to Drop Kick Murphy—as long as nobody's cranking any country. Other than that, he says, he'll ride to just about anything.

Considering his long and strong career and unwavering dedication to the sport, we're willing to second-guess that. If you see him, drop some country--we suspect he'll just ride anyway.

Lynda Twardowski is a Los Angeles-based freelance writer specializing in lifestyle and outdoor-recreation features. She has contributed to numerous books for teens.

MOTOCROSS

MOTO

CROSS

Flipped Out

Of all the "extreme" sports featured in this book, the most profoundly dangerous, and therefore arguably the most extreme, is motocross. Whether it's through outrageous freestyle jumps or balls-out super-cross, nowhere are competitors going huge, and injuring themselves more spectacularly, than on motocross bikes.

Consider the evidence. Young Travis Pastrana has suffered through 12 surgeries, over 30 broken bones, and 10 concussions. An out-of-whack back and injuries to both arms conspired to keep Jeremy McGrath from the top of the American Motocross Association (AMA) heap in 2002. In 2000 Jeremy Max Paget, a promising young rider, was killed after short-landing a jump at a race in Utah. In January 2002 Mark Anderson, president of the Arizona Oldtimers MX Club, was killed in a Grand Prix. The list goes on and on.

The point is not to condemn motocross as too dangerous—riders by and large know the risks they run every time they strap a power of 100 horses between their legs and go sailing into the stratosphere. The point is this: why is something so dangerous so popular?

Perhaps it has something to do with the same motivations that brought hordes of Romans into the Coliseum to watch gladiators compete in blood sport, or to cheer as the Christians were fed to the lions. It seems that even 2000 years ago few things were more exciting than lining up for an event where someone might die.

But there's even more to it. Motocross is simply, mind bogglingly spectacular to watch. Whether it's Jeremy McGrath or Ricky Carmichael and a crew of hellmen blasting around a course and through the air in a supercross event, or an occasionally healthy Travis Pastrana pulling a backflip over a 50-foot gap, the aerial fireworks are jaw dropping. When motocrossers make it, they make it in spectacular fashion. When they eat it, they quite literally might die.

Is it our blood lust that draws us to the events? Or is it the promise of speed and spectacle? It's probably a little bit of both.

In 2002 the AMA Supercross Series was second only to NASCAR in motorsports spectator attendance. And it seems that the more extreme it gets, the more it just keeps growing by leaps and bounds. The X Games begat the Gravity Games, and freestyle moto, once the bastard stepchild of supercross, has become the new darling of the Games.

In the following pages we'll profile supercross legend Jeremy McGrath, freestyle radical Brian Deegan, and young ripper Travis Pastrana, who somehow manages to bridge the gap between the two. Each rider has helped define what motocross is in the new millennium, and each will likely go a long way in defining where the sport goes in the future. That is if they can keep from killing themselves.

—Chris Dixon

CAREY HART COMPETES IN THE 2000 GRAVITY
GAMES IN PROVIDENCE, RHODE ISLAND.

Travis Pastrana

BORN: ANNAPOLIS, MARYLAND
BIRTH DATE: OCTOBER 8, 1983
HEIGHT: 6'2"
WEIGHT: 170 POUNDS
RESIDENCE: ANNAPOLIS, MARYLAND
MARITAL STATUS: SINGLE

Travis Pastrana is probably smarter than you are. It's very likely that he is also faster, braver, and quite a bit more insane than you as well.

How else could this kid, who is now only 18 years old, have been U.S. amateur champion five times from 1992 to 1998? How else could he have won a world freestyle championship at age 14, then take an X Games gold medal *and* graduate from high school at age 15? How else could he be a 4.0 student at the University of Maryland? And how the hell else could he also have completed over 100 successful backflips within the first couple of months of beginning to attempt them in 2002?

Maybe it's in the genes. Maybe it's luck. Maybe it's in a simple love for what he's doing. Whatever it is, Pastrana is a wonder kid, both on the bike and off.

When he was just four years old, Travis' dad gave him his first bike, a Honda Z-50. On a backyard track, the kid began to hone his skills and by his early teenage years, he was becoming a giant killer on race and freestyle circuits on his 125cc Suzuki.

Despite being at the top of his game at an incredibly young age, Pastrana's career was nearly ended in 1998 when he was involved in a frightful accident that literally dislocated his spinal column from his pelvis in a practice run at the Free Air Festival in Lake Havasu, California. This sort of accident usually results in paralysis, but thanks to being in incredible shape at the time of the crash, Pastrana was only confined to a wheelchair for a few months.

Fully recovered in 1999, Pastrana went ballistic at the inaugural Moto X competition at the San Francisco X Games. After pulling an outrageous "Rodeo Air" (a move in which both legs are over the bars and only one hand is holding on) and several no-handed landings, the young airman scored a 99 out of 100 and took gold.

Thoroughly stoked after his high score, Pastrana made action-sports history, and every major news channel, by jumping his bike 100 feet into the waters of San Francisco Bay. Of course, he was promptly arrested. "We didn't plan it, and we didn't tell anybody," he said afterwards.

Other highlights of 1999 included gold at the Gravity Games and a victory in his first ever 125cc pro race. That the kid could excel in both disciplines shows his phenomenal crossover talent.

Which does he like better, Supercross or Freestyle motocross? "I have more fun in Supercross, because there are so many more options. You really have a lot more options with different jumps and things, whereas in motocross your only chance for creativity is through different lines."

From his results, you wouldn't know he had a favorite.

During the 2000 season, Pastrana's results were nothing short of extraordinary, and included wins in Daytona, St. Louis, and the

East/West shootout in Supercross, and gold in the Summer X Games Moto X. Not surprisingly, Pastrana was named AMA Rookie of the Year.

Pastrana attributes some of his rookie success and riding style to a pair of nonmotorized sports he also loves: BMX and mountain biking. In an interview with his best friend and fellow rider Stephane Roncada, Pastrana spoke about the influence BMX has on his riding style. "I definitely like to ride my BMX bike and watch the contests, and I can do some of the dirt jumping and

other racers have long since left the signing tables. The kid seems to instinctively realize what an effect a positive role model can have on aspiring riders. He pointed this out when talking about one of his own heroes. "I think that Doug Henry is probably my biggest influence in motocross," he says. "I was 10 years old when I first met him, and he was the only guy who really took the time to talk to me. He's a great guy and a great racer."

Talking of his first year running with the pros, Pastrana was humble. "It started out rough," he said, "with a lot of crashes, and

"It started out rough, with a lot of crashes. At the same time, though, I realized that I had the speed to run with those guys and that's really what it took: a little confidence."

things, but honestly I am really bad on a bicycle. I try, but I always seem to get hurt on the things."

In fact, he had just broken his leg on a BMX a few months prior to the interview.

Despite the broken bones, and though he is clearly one of the most extreme riders in the sport, Pastrana is not one to try to define his life by being your typical punk kid motocross rider. In fact, Pastrana has made a name for himself since his childhood by being one heck of a nice kid and by letting his riding, rather than his attitude, do the talking.

His life is essentially 180 degrees opposite from that of continuous rival Brian Deegan and his crew of "Metal Mulisha" crackpots. Pastrana has been known to sit signing autographs and greeting fans for hours after

everything that comes with coming into the pros. At the same time, I realized that I had the speed to run with those guys and that's really what it took: a little bit of confidence."

In 2001 Pastrana's career was marked by more victories but also by a string of serious injuries that had many questioning whether Supercross and his sponsors were more interested in selling tickets and bikes than in the safety of its riders. In January 2001, right after healing from his broken leg, Pastrana suffered a Grade 3 concussion during an AMA Supercross event in San Diego. A Grade 3 is defined as a serious head trauma caused by an impact that literally causes the brain to bounce around in the skull.

A week later Pastrana attempted to ride again, but bowed out due to residual dizziness from the concussion. At Unadilla,

New York, Pastrana was knocked out and suffered another concussion following a crash, which forced him to give up a hard-fought lead at the very end of the race.

One concussion can result in permanent brain damage. During 2001 Pastrana was said to have suffered five. Despite these injuries, Pastrana finished the season as the Eastern 125cc champion and ESPN's Motocross Rider of the Year.

At the 2000 Gravity Games, hellman Carey Hart let off a "Shot Heard Round the World" with a complete backflip. The backflip is a

hauling ass around a rally course in Europe in a $1 million Subaru rally car—all in the last year.

Today Pastrana is pulling flips off ramps and over 50-foot gaps, and it appears that the sky is the limit. Still, it's one thing to be a hell-bent teenager pulling flips without a thought, quite another to be a worried mother. But Travis' mother, Debbie, seems to be taking her son's new obsession in stride.

"I think Travis can backflip better than he can walk," she says, "He just looks like he's in complete control doing a backflip. I get

Staying healthy is a tall order given the stress of competition, the need to stay in phenomenal shape, and the need to continually push into treacherous maneuvers at frightening speeds.

staggeringly dangerous maneuver since it's so easy to have your 100-plus pound bike land on you, or for you to land on your head if you screw it up.

Of his own first successful attempt, Pastrana had this to say: "It scared me to death. I mean, it just doesn't make sense. You're still on your motorcycle at the height of the jump going, 'This thing's not going to rotate around.' I knew it was possible. It just doesn't seem logical."

It's amazing that a young man who makes such fearless moves on a bike claims to be so prone to motion sickness that he can't ride a roller-coaster or be in a car and read at the same time. That hasn't stopped him, though, from getting certified for sky-diving, performing an 80 mph parachute-assisted flip into the Grand Canyon on a motorbike, and

nervous watching him 30 feet in the air hanging off the back of the bike, but the backflip looks so smooth."

Though he's had an extreme year, 2002 has proved to be a difficult one for young Pastrana. Not because he can't ride with the best of them, but because he can't seem to stay healthy.

In July he was just getting a cast off from a broken wrist while also battling a recurring sinus infection that had sapped his strength for months. The infections became so chronic that Travis ended up having his tonsils taken out. On top of that he battled mononucleosis, Epstein Barr virus, and a frightening disease called parvo. According to Pastrana, "It's a disease dogs get. They don't even have a record of humans getting it. You can actually get it from eating dirt, which I've done a lot of lately."

For the young Mr. Nice Guy, getting and staying healthy will be the keys to future success in both Supercross and Freestyle. Pastrana has broken over 20 bones to date, and staying healthy is a tall order given the stress of so many competitions, the need to stay in phenomenal shape, and the need to continually push into treacherous maneuvers at frightening speeds. Such is the nature of today's motocross.

Should Pastrana manage to keep himself relatively free of injury and illness, he will, in all likelihood, become one of the legends of the sport. It couldn't happen to a nicer kid.

"I just keep it fun, and give it my all," he says. "How could I not keep going when I'm making a living doing something I love?"

Brian Deegan

BORN: OMAHA, NEBRASKA
BIRTH DATE: MAY 9, 1975
HEIGHT: 5'9"
WEIGHT: 165 POUNDS
RESIDENCE: TEMECULA, CALIFORNIA
MARITAL STATUS: SINGLE
CHILDREN: 1

If you have read anything written about Brian Deegan in the last few years, you might have come to the conclusion that he was a jerk, or a punk. You might call him a redneck, or perhaps a moron. You could also think him a hero who tells it like it is. Or maybe you'd realize that he's all of the above, and one hell of a smart businessman to boot.

Businessman? Yes, much in the spirit of a brilliant musician and marketer named Marilyn Manson, Brian Deegan has found fame, fortune, and a paycheck in pushing people's buttons and saying and doing outrageous things. Oh, and in jumping his Honda like a man possessed.

Deegan was born in the flatlands of Omaha, Nebraska, in 1975 and started riding a Honda 50cc dirt bike at the ripe old age of 10. Like many kids, he rode for fun, but after a while he found he was good at it and decided to start competing.

In 1996 Deegan signed on to race supercross with the Chapparal team. But he and another Supercross friend named Larry Linkogle immediately became unhappy with the rules and constraints that came with being a factory rider. That was the beginning of the Metal Mulisha.

"I sold out when I signed my contract with Chaparral," says Deegan. "You sell out when there are clauses in your contract telling you what you can and can't do. Selling out doesn't mean riding for a sponsor; selling out is when you let a sponsor tell you what to do."

Deegan and Linkogle started the Mulisha as a haven for the misfits of the sport. "Motocross has turned absolutely pussy because of all these glamrock, fag, factory geeks," he says. "We couldn't handle hanging out with all the factory geeks any more, with their fluorescent clothes and their bleached hair and all their fancy jewelry and cars.

"Everyone came down on me and Larry because we're punks and all we like to do is ride our dirt bikes. So we decided to name our group of punks and misfits the Metal Mulisha to bring back the old-school attitude of dirtbikes. You know—death, danger, and all that evil s---. We had to do it before it turned completely bulls---.

"After years of the magazines and corporate geeks bashing our lifestyle," he continued, "the Mulisha has a following of the sickest athletes associated with freeriding. Like it or not, freestyle is taking over. And we have set new limits so that freeriders can be as gnarly as they want, with the freedom to do and say anything they want."

If you've read or seen any interviews with Deegan, you'd know that the young man practices what he preaches, and he doesn't much care whether you agree with him or not. "I'm not out to be a punk or a fake person," he says. "If people don't like me, they don't like me, and if they don't, I don't really care."

It would be easy to dismiss Deegan as nothing more than a loudmouth were it not for the fact that the Metal Mulisha has

created such a following—and if Deegan and crew didn't back up their words with some of the ballsiest freeriding in the world. If you look at the Mulisha's popularity over the past few years, you could, of course, cite the fact that everyone loves to be identified with the rebels. That's how most rock stars make their millions.

But there's something more subtle, and just as important, at work here. One of the facts of modern motorsports—be they auto, boat, or motorcycle--is that the machines of today are so sophisticated and expensive that to

Suicide." In the jump Deegan pulled a double can-can with his right hand off the bike and landed with both legs on one side of the bike—sidesaddle. It was a sick jump that left absolutely no margin for error.

Deegan named the trick after a song by Slayer. "I think it threw a lot of people off and they weren't ready for it. This is my mentality. I don't care how big the jump is, I'll go for it."

Part of the reason the jump earned gold for Deegan was because no one expected it. "I didn't tell anyone about it," he continues. "I didn't tell my manager. S---, I didn't even tell

"Go ahead and say I'm a sellout. I'll be in my five-bedroom house, swimming in my pool, jumping my dirt bike, and riding my Harley-Davidson into town.

compete at a high level you simply have to be a factory rider. This also means that the factory puts tons of money behind you and expects you to pay that back in good behavior.

The difference with freeriding is, with the exception of needing a powerful motor and a reasonable suspension, any bike can be used for freestyle—and thus, any kid who's a talented jumper can do well without having to follow the rules of the factory. Thus, many of the factory freeriders, and particularly the members of Deegan's Metal Mulisha, can pretty much do and say what they want, as long as they keep pulling off their insane jumps.

And make no mistake, the jumps are totally insane.

At the 2002 Winter X Games, Deegan pulled a 100-foot jump called a "Mandatory

my dad. I think this is up there with the most difficult tricks I've ever done."

Like most renowned bike jumpers, the most difficult tricks have left Deegan with scores of injuries. Still, he keeps on jumping. "I've had a lot of surgeries, and I've had a lot of rods and pins in my body. I broke my back; I broke my arms. I've been through all the s---."

He's hit his head quite a bit too. "I've had a lot of concussions, and a lot of memory loss. I think I'm half retarded sometimes from my concussions. I'm kinda just lost, you know. Half the time I'm just picking at things, screwing around, and just kinda trip out. It's pretty cool actually, because that way I have an excuse for all the dumb s--- I do."

Like many motorippers, Deegan feels that his livelihood is just about the most dangerous way to make a living on the planet. "I think you should be paid," he says, "based on how gnarly your sport is. Motocross is by far the gnarliest sport so it's got the gnarliest injuries. I watch TV and see these basketball guys fall on the ground and they cry, and they obviously get paid well compared to when we crash. It just cracks me up."

Of the Metal Mulisha, Deegan claims that it has grown far beyond his expectations. Members now include not only freestylers like Jeremy Steinberg, Colin Morrison, and Ronnie "Kung Fu" Faisst, but also guys like bare-knuckle ultimate fighter John the "Machine" Lober. "It's grown so fast I think we've almost lost control of what it is right now," says Deegan. "It's almost like a motorcycle gang, but I kinda like where it's going, out of our hands."

But is it real rebellion, or just good business? Maybe it's a little bit of both. Take his revenue from the Mulisha, contests, and sponsors like Hansen's energy drinks, and Deegan is a rich young man. And he doesn't really care if you call him a sellout.

"Go ahead and say I'm a sellout," he says. "I'll just be in my five-bedroom house, swimming in my pool, jumping my dirt bike, and riding my Harley-Davidson into town. Money is great, and anyone who says winning a lot of money is bad has mental problems. Making money allows me to make a living at what I want to do. I was poor once, and that wasn't cool."

Fellow ripper Travis Pastrana has his own opinions on Deegan and the Mulisha. "It's more than an act for Deegan," says Pastrana. "It's his life. And I don't want to blow it for him, but deep down inside Deegan is really a nice guy. I don't think it's great for the sport, but he's doing really well with it, as far as the

business side is concerned. He's making big profits off of it. It was funny, at the X Games he pulled up to the high-jump competition with an open-faced helmet and a cigarette in his mouth. I was like, 'Brian, what the heck are you doing? That's terrible for the kids in our sport.' Brian said, 'Dude, just watch this—the media is going to eat this up. I'll be front cover on every single magazine out there!' He is really a nice guy, though, and smart when it comes to making money."

When asked by his friend and fellow racer Stephane Roncada whether he would ever join the Mulisha, Pastrana replied, "No, I would never go to the Mulisha because of what it stands for. My parents would kill me!"

For his own part Deegan probably doesn't mind if Pastrana joins or not. It just means more girls and more glory for him.

But he does believe he has some responsibility toward the kids who would seek to emulate him on the dirt. As Deegan said, "Anyone getting into dirtbikes and freestyle, you've gotta go out and build a good background before you try the stuff we're doing. It's not something you learn overnight. So for all the kids out there, go out and practice some jumps first before you try any of the stuff that we do."

Brian Deegan is enjoying life, making friends, and making enemies on his own terms. Which is more than you can say for most folks. If you don't like him, fine, he'll still go on doing what he's doing: blowing minds and blowing things up until his fast-lane life catches up with him in some way or another.

"Live your own life," he says, "and take a lot of chances. Go out there, because you only live once. That's the story of my life, and so far, I'm still livin'."

MOTOCROSS TERMS

AERIALS

ANY OF A VARIETY OF WAYS OF HUCKING A MOTORCYCLE INTO THE AIR.

BAIL

TO THROW YOUR BIKE AWAY FROM YOUR BODY BEFORE A CRASH. SOME PEOPLE ALSO REFER TO A CRASH AS A BAIL.

BAR HOP

ARMS HOLD THE BAR WHILE BOTH FEET GO BETWEEN THEM AND OVER THE FRONT FENDER DURING A JUMP.

BEATER

A CRASH.

CAN-CAN

RIDER LIFTS ONE LEG OVER THE BIKE TO THE SIDE AND BACK BEFORE LANDING.

CANDY BAR

SKETCHY JUMP PERFORMED WITH ONE LEG OVER THE BARS AND FOOT ON FRONT FENDER.

CLIFFHANGER

DURING A JUMP, THE RIDER HOOKS HIS FEET UNDER THE HANDLEBARS AND RAISES HIS HANDS IN THE AIR.

COFFIN

A JUMP MOVE PERFORMED WHEN THE RIDER LAYS BACK ON THE SEAT WHILE STILL HOLDING THE BARS.

CORDOVA

DANGEROUS, DISORIENTING JUMP IN WHICH RIDER HOOKS HIS FEET UNDER THE HANDLEBARS AND DOES A REVERSE BACK ARCH UNTIL HE IS LOOKING UPSIDE DOWN AND BEHIND HIM.

DIALED-IN

TO HAVE YOUR BIKE OR YOUR RIDING METHOD IN PERFECT WORKING ORDER.

DOUBLE CAN-CAN

JUMP MOVE DONE BY PUTTING ONE LEG TO THE OPPOSITE SIDE OF THE BIKE, BRINGING THE OTHER LEG TO MEET IT, AND RAISING YOUR BUTT OFF THE SEAT.

HART ATTACK

NAMED FOR RIDER CAREY HART. A SEAT GRAB JUMP WITH LEGS PUSHED STRAIGHT UP IN THE AIR.

HEEL CLICKER

RIDER BRINGS BOTH FEET OFF THE PEGS AND TOUCHES THEM TOGETHER OVER THE HANDLEBARS.

INDIAN AIR

A SUPERMAN SEAT-GRAB JUMP WITH A LEG CROSS THROWN IN.

NAC-NAC

JUMP IN WHICH A RIDER BRINGS ONE LEG OVER THE REAR OF THE BIKE TO APPEAR THAT HE'S GETTING OFF THE BIKE IN MIDAIR. PERFECTED BY JEREMY MCGRATH.

NO-HANDER LANDER

JUST WHAT IT SAYS—LANDING A JUMP WITH NO HANDS. VERY DANGEROUS AND CURRENTLY VERY POPULAR.

RODEO AIR

HEEL-CLICKER JUMP LANDED WITH ONE HAND IN THE CENTER OF THE HANDLEBARS AND THE OTHER RAISED OVER THE HEAD LIKE A BULL RIDER.

SUPERMAN

JUMP IN WHICH RIDER LIFTS LEGS FROM THE PEGS AND THROWS THEM OVER THE BACK OF THE BIKE TO APPEAR THAT HE IS FLYING.

source: expn.com

Jeremy McGrath

BORN: SAN FRANCISCO, CALIFORNIA
BIRTH DATE: NOVEMBER 19, 1971
HEIGHT: 5'10"
WEIGHT: 165 POUNDS
RESIDENCE: MURRIETA, CALIFORNIA
MARITAL STATUS: SINGLE

In November 1971 Jack and Ann McGrath brought a boy into the world and named him Jeremy. They raised him with love, discipline, and attention, and then one day when he was six years old, Jack put Jeremy on a motorcycle. Thus was born the "Chosen One."

The young Chosen One was a very fortunate child. Not only was his dad a motocross racer himself, but he also supported everything his son did. Jeremy rode with his dad on family land outside of San Francisco pretty much whenever he wanted, and was given his own first bike, a YZ80, in 1985.

Since dad was also a mechanic, young Jeremy learned everything about how motocross bikes work. Riding his Yamaha and perfecting his jumping techniques on a BMX bike, the kid began to show serious promise as a rider. He entered his first race in June 1986 and worked in a Honda shop and as a grocery-store bag boy to support his early efforts.

Like most kids, he had idols—Rick Johnson, Damon Bradshaw, David Baily, and Johnny O'Mara, to name a few. Unlike most kids, he started seriously emulating them on the track. "I still have that childhood image of seeing all those guys as my heroes," he says, "and I idolized them. They were the baddest, and to me, they always will be the baddest."

In 1989 McGrath made the leap into professional racing, and finished eighth in the AMA Western Regional Supercross Series. He began turning heads almost immediately with an incredibly smooth and precise riding style that won races and left him with very few injuries. While other racers were working out, watching their diets, and training religiously, all McGrath did was ride, ride, ride. His results were nothing short of astonishing.

In 1991 McGrath won the Western Regional Supercross title. He repeated the feat in 1992, then stunned the world in 1993 by taking the National Supercross championship in his rookie season—an almost unimaginable feat. "When I eventually turned to the 250 class in 1993," he says, "it took me a few races to kind of feel my way around. But once I won the first race, that was the turning point and then I just started dominating.

To say he started dominating is almost an understatement. Between 1991 and 2000 McGrath *killed it*. He won a record seven Supercross titles and changed the very face and nature of the sport. Like Tony Hawk, McGrath came into a sport practiced by the devoted and the hardcore, who do what they do not for the money, but for the adrenaline.

Motocrossing dwelt on the fringes in the desert southwest and the mud-bogs of the southeast. But through sheer, mind-blowing talent, business sense, and willpower, McGrath led Supercross into a period of explosive growth. Like Michael Jordan, McGrath has dominated the sport as no one before him, becoming a one-man media miracle.

The legacy of his success can be seen in the ever-increasing television coverage and attendance of supercross events; in the number of video games featuring virtual McGraths, Pastranas, and Deegans; in action figures and remote-control toys; and in the simply mind-boggling money now being thrown at top young riders.

When asked about his success, McGrath says, "The toughest question to answer is how come I've been so successful. Truthfully, I don't know what sets me apart. I just have

his dream. "All I ever dreamed of as a kid was to get to the supercross tracks," he says, "just to be able to ride in front of the fans, and ride those stadium tracks."

In spite of it all, McGrath doesn't necessarily feel famous. "It's really hard for me to get the feeling because I'm Jeremy McGrath. I don't see everyone, like the fans, the swarming, or the idolization that the kids get. I know how I felt when I had a hero, but being that guy is a lot different. Your friends or your family or someone else can tell you how big it

"Truthfully, I don't know what sets me apart. I just have always liked to ride and challenge myself. I'm just real competitive at whatever I do, and I really, really like to ride motorcycles. The minute I don't have fun, I'll stop."

always liked to ride and challenge myself. I'm just real competitive at whatever I do, and I really, really like to ride motorcycles."

And maybe that's the point. Despite literally millions in endorsement deals, and being far and away the richest man on two wheels, McGrath's motivating force is still fun. "I'm really not in it for the money," he says. "I know that it's hard to understand because I'm always working on new deals and won't race unless it's in my contract or I get really good show-up money. But those are things I need to do to protect my interests. I'm really not fixated on making money, and I never want to be that way. In the long run, it's not about money—it's about fun. The minute I don't have fun, I'll stop."

That it's so much fun is evident to anyone who talks to a young man who is clearly living

is, but I really don't notice."

Jeremy runs his empire with the help of his friends and family, especially his mother, best buddy Jeff Surwall, and manager Dave Stephenson. Everyone contributes to the success of McGrath, Inc. Duties includes publicity; dealing with media interviews with magazines like *Playboy* and appearances on shows like *The Tonight Show*; and overseeing things like action figures, remote-control toys, and video deals. And then there is dealing with a dizzying array of contractual and sponsor obligations.

"I can hardly do anything without it violating one contract or another," McGrath says, "and I think that I'm in the best position of anyone. I've had a video-game sponsor for a couple of years [his first video-game appearance came way back in 1998]. Now another video-game company comes in and is going to sponsor the [race] series, and I'm sponsored by a different video-game company."

This sort of thing invariably leads to one company calling foul against the other over something as seemingly simple as sticker placement. But sticker and logo placement mean everything when you're Jeremy McGrath, and he's got a limited amount of very expensive real estate on his clothes and bike. On several occasions sponsors have expected McGrath to sport the stickers of competing companies side by side.

As a result, no one ends up happy. "This kind of political stuff bothers me," he says.

When asked about the explosion in freestyle riding, McGrath has plenty to say, even giving props to antagonist Brian Deegan. "At first," says McGrath, "it was kind of a shady deal because it was all the rebel type of guys out there doing it. I think it is going good with the X Games and Gravity Games, and Travis Pastrana is a good role model. He's a kid, he's happy to be there, and he's not all into the ego thing. I think those guys ride great; they just need to mellow it out and just get along. They need to help us promote motocross, and then they'll get a lot more backing from motocross."

McGrath doesn't find most freestyle riding all that extreme. "The guys get my respect on the riding, but I don't think that it's 'extreme' riding. I don't think that jumping a ramp and doing tricks is extreme riding."

When asked if he would like to compete in freestyle, McGrath responds that he likes the competition of racing. "I personally don't like the thought of being judged; there is a lot of politics in that. A sport like motocross or

supercross is competition; the first guy to the finish line wins. I like that better."

Still, he definitely thinks several freestylists are "sick." "Carey Hart and Mike Metzger are awesome. Those guys are going crazy, and Travis Pastrana is insane. Even Brian Deegan is going off now. It's just the other part of their lifestyle that is real weird to understand."

McGrath is pretty happy with his own lifestyle up to now. Despite injuries, he still managed to finish third overall in the 2002 supercross season. In August 2002 he finally married his longtime sweetheart Kim Maddox, moving him forward into the next phase of his life—a phase that he hopes will soon lead to a family of his own.

And in spite of all that he's accomplished, the wily veteran is still thankful for those who put him where he is. "I'll stay there hours upon hours doing autographs," he says. "Especially the kids, I really love the kids. I think the fans realize that I appreciate everything that they do for me and it pays off for me in the end as well."

Should he stay healthy, McGrath feels he still has several more solid years of racing ahead of him, and believes himself strong enough to one day claim supercross championship number eight. "I am still hungry," he says, "and I want to win."

But even if he doesn't, he seems to be pretty satisfied with the life he's made for himself. "No matter what happens," he says, "even if I don't win another race again, I think I'm one of the luckiest guys in the world."

Chris Dixon is a Laguna Beach, California, based freelance writer who contributes to Surfer *magazine,* The New York Times, *and various other publications.*

On a Roll

In 1994 rollerblading was about riding down stairs, leaping over trash cans, and seeing how much speed you could get by bombing down hills. We wore Dr. Bone Saver kneepads, wrist guards, and baggy shorts hanging beyond our knees.

The sport's trick vocabulary list was minimal and competition was almost nonexistent. We were simply trying to do something other than just rolling around the lake or down long, winding roads leading nowhere. We wanted everyone to know we were more than just kids on skates.

Ideas and concepts slowly began to piece themselves together. Companies began to pop up in random parts of the country, with the hub of skating centered in the state of California.

Focus was put on wheels, grind plates, frames, and the overall appearance of the skate. By changing the look we ultimately detached ourselves from the everyday inline skater stereotype and created an identity all our own. Each company (Rollerblade, Roces, Scribe, Senate, and Cozmo to name a few) searched for strong teams to help create their identity.

With any lifestyle, creating an identity is valuable. It helps define a team and pieces together the distinguished personalities for its foundation. Each team, whether wheel, skate, or grind plate, had its own mission and statement.

It was videos that let the world—especially the early pioneers who would soon take the sport to new levels—know that inline skating was more than just a leisurely activity. Companies in California could find hidden talent in states like Minnesota, Nebraska, New York, Florida, and Texas. Videos like *Dare to Air*, *Mad Beef*, *Videogroove*, and the *Hoax* series allowed kids to see skaters like Chris Edwards, Arlo Eisenberg, Brooke Howard Smith, Steve Thomas, B-Love, Dave Kollasch, and many more. They were the visionaries and leaders—a handful of personalities that laid the foundation and opened the innovative window that has let kids use their imaginations and talent to the fullest extent as they roll along on eight wheels.

Every sport has leaders—not just people who push the envelope, but people who push a sport forward by creating media outlets and giving back to a lifestyle that they helped assemble. Today we have many inline leaders, and they're putting their energy into magazines, companies, and grassroots tours to help strengthen the sport and make sure it continues in a positive direction. Some are team managers while others happen to be commentators for big events like the Gravity Games and X Games. Some produce video magazines, put together pro tours, own skate shops, or use their imaginative eye to photograph the timeline of moments and events that take place within our select industry.

GERMANY'S BRUNO LOWE LOOKS
DOWN DURING A RUN IN THE MEN'S
AGGRESSIVE INLINE PARK SKATE ON
AUGUST 16, 2002, DURING THE X
GAMES IN PHILADELPHIA.

It is now 2002. The talent pool is overflowing like a bowl of cheerios. Kids between the ages of 13 and 19 have begun their artistic assault on inline skates and the concrete playground this country has to offer.

There are too many names to mention, and too many innovators to document. Chris Haffey, Aaron Feinberg, Brian Shima, Carlos Pianowski, and Randy Spizer will stand strong in the street-skating side of things. With vert skating, names like Takeshi Yasutoko, Taig Khris, Shane Yost, and Fabiola da Silva will be etched into the history books of aggressive inline skating forever. But please note, this list is just a small fraction of the many imaginative people who pull tricks that were deemed impractical years ago. It's evolving that quickly.

The trick vocabulary has advanced as rapidly as the talent within this industry. Back in 1994 the short list of tricks included frontsides, backsides, mizous, soul grinds, royales, top souls, and trying to pull 180s, 360s, and 540s while going down small sets of stairs. But with every sport the imagination expands and the level of creativity continues to broaden when you see others pushing themselves and testing their limits on magic boots.

Today kids are spinning 540 into grinds, doing rails with 30-foot drop-offs, and using obstacles, ledges, and the ground with a whole new frame of mind. It's hard to find limitations when you have a variety of fearless individuals who use imagination and focus as their key ingredients to stand out from the masses.

Exposure to this lifestyle has been captured on national television with pro-sanctioned events like the Aggressive Skaters Association (ASA). Pro riders can make good money by competing all over the country for top honors at street and vert competitions.

Furthermore, ESPN and NBC now host the X Games and Gravity Games and put up hefty purses for inline skating and other action-sports lifestyles. But it doesn't stop there.

Within the last year or so an organization called IMYTA (I Match Your Trick Association) has touched down and recreated the true essence of what street skating is to our subculture. For they say freedom discovers human beings the moment we lose concern over what impression we are making. Contests on the streets of California, Michigan, England, France, Minnesota, and Atlanta have brought together our street culture and reminded us that art reaches its greatest peak when devoid of self-consciousness. The movement is being documented on DVD by *Videogroove* magazine.

We are falling back to our roots—the days when we just went rolling with our friends for fun and adventure, not necessarily for fame and notoriety. New magazines, websites, online skate shops, and video magazines remind us that we are still strong and moving forward.

That's youth for you. We set our own limits without even asking our body and mind if they can take it. Yet the body and mind always do.

—*Jeff Erdmann*

Jeff Erdmann is a Minneapolis-based freelance writer specializing in inline skating. He is the managing editor of Rejects *magazine, former editor of* Box *magazine, former online editor for the Gravity Games, and a contributor to* Daily Bread *magazine and* Bluetorch.com.

Cheap Thrills

It was tantamount to winter-sports war when snowboarders first began infiltrating ski slopes with their quirky brand of one-planked churning several years ago. "Just who are these punks," skiers cried, "and why don't they test their rebel-rousing hijinks somewhere else?"

The result of these feuds was the banning of snowboarders from many of the country's prime hills, and in some places it continues today.

Wakeboarding's transition toward acceptance was far easier. In fact, the one-plank variety of the popular sport of water skiing was quickly embraced for its awesome visual impact and for its fast learning curve—at least compared to other board sports.

For starters, wakeboarding expenses are virtually nil once you get a board, gain access to water, and find somebody with a boat. And while you are being pulled at roughly 20 miles per hour and can elevate as high as 15 feet above the surface, tumbling on water is far more appealing than biting it on concrete, asphalt, or even snow.

A sure indication of wakeboarding's staying power came in 1996 when it was chosen as a sport in that year's X Games. Thanks largely to Lake Alfred, Florida, resident Parks Bonifay, wakeboarding didn't disappoint. Bonifay dazzled onlookers with a stunning array of flips, spins, turns, and jumps. Only 14 years old at the time, Bonifay walked away with the inaugural X Games gold medal and to this day leads the sport in creativity and moxie.

BMX has its miracle boy in Dave Mirra; in Bonifay, wakeboarding found its wonder boy—an apt nickname that has stuck ever since Bonifay entered the *Guinness Book of World Records* as the youngest water skier ever at six months and 29 days.

Bonifay, a fixture on the pro circuit since 1994, prides himself on being a versatile competitor. "Judges don't just want to see kids go out there and do flips all the way down and back," Bonifay insists. "They're looking for variety."

The endless variety of tricks is just one reason for wakeboarding's widespread popularity. Another major draw is its availability to anyone with a desire to be dragged across the water on a board. Unlike surfing, which in the continental U.S. is mainly reserved for those who have access to the massive swells of the Pacific Ocean, waves don't play a huge role in wakeboarding.

For example, Florida (land of the smaller waves) is home to many of the top pros, including Bonifay, Ricky Gonzales, Danny Harf, as well as top women competitors Tara Hamilton, Meaghan Majors, and Dallas Friday.

Friday may have the perfect name for a detective show character of yesteryear, but she's very much where wakeboarding is going. She joined the pro circuit in 2000 at the ripe old age of 13 and immediately made waves by winning that year's America's Cup

Championship, finishing second at the X Games, third at the National Wakeboarding Championships, and fourth at the Gravity Games. Given her youth, gender, and amazing achievements, Friday is the perfect spokes-person for the all-inclusive nature of wakeboarding.

"Wakeboarding is all about having fun," said Friday, who won the 2001 Gravity Games and finished first in her preliminary heat in the 2002 edition in Cleveland, Ohio. "If you lose your focus of having fun and take things too seriously, you put unwanted stress on yourself and cannot possibly enjoy it. I

PARKS BONIFAY

always try to have fun even when I train every day."

If Friday is the future of women's wakeboarding, Tara Hamilton helped put the sport on the map. Hamilton dominated her first three years as a pro from 1997–1999. In 1997 alone she claimed the World

Championship, the Pro Wakeboarding Tour title, and the X Games gold medal. Although she finished 2000 as the top-ranked woman, a stress fracture to her right heel in 2001 forced her to miss some competition. Many believe that injury led to the demise of her dominance.

Hamilton, who has since lost her number one world ranking, stresses a well-rounded approach to life, an ethos echoed by many professional and recreational wakeboarders. She discussed this in a 2000 interview, about the time the rest of the wakeboarding world began to catch up to her.

"This is my fourth season, and I am concentrating on graduating and getting ready for college," said Hamilton, then a high school senior. "So my thoughts are not always on wakeboarding.

"The other girls are making it hard for me to keep my number one spot, but that's good for the sport and that is what competition is all about. They are still pretty new at all the traveling stuff, so it hasn't worn in yet. But overall it's good and I have great sponsors. I personally think I have the best sponsors in the industry."

But the beauty of wakeboarding is that you don't have to have Mountain Dew, Ford, or Vans (just a few of Hamilton's gaggle of sponsors) to fall back on to enjoy the sport. All you need is a boat, a board, a driver—and a desire to fly across the water on a single plank.

—*Aaron George*

Aaron George is a Chicago-based freelance writer and former editor of Core Sports *magazine.* He has written numerous feature articles on action sports.

Addictive Behavior

Desirable surfing conditions are so rare that a truly committed surfer tends to put life on hold when the waves turn on. This seemingly flaky sense of priorities can be difficult for nonsurfers to understand, especially the disappointed boss and/or spouse of said missing surfer.

Simply put, surfing is highly addictive. All it takes is one good wave to get hooked for life.

Especially irresistible are waves that enable tube riding—the most sought-after aspect of surfing. Tube rides occur when the lip of the wave pitches out over your head, momentarily encasing you dryly in a cylinder of water. Time seemingly slows down in the tube as your senses explode in a state of super-heightened awareness.

Once inside, the challenge is to stay on your board and keep it angled toward the exit while maintaining enough speed to make it out unscathed. Once out, the aim is to carve a speedy arc back around toward the pocket and set up for another trip through the tube.

On those ultrarare days when quality tube-riding conditions occur in any beach town, a certain percentage of the local work force will not show up at their jobs. "Never hire a surfer," remarked a knowing real-estate investor during an extraordinarily well-shaped day in Newport Beach, California.

Like all addicts, the surf junkie will do whatever it takes to score a fix. Bogus excuses such as, "My aunt died," are common. However, not all surfers operate with a total lack of integrity. Some will at least not phone their boss with such "news" without first squashing a black ant dead in its tracks with a fingertip. And of course some truly responsible surfers do exist who'll actually bite the bullet and faithfully show up for work no matter how good the surf is.

But the truly fortunate are the handful of surfers out there who don't have to worry about calling in sick to go surfing because they've somehow managed to make surfing their full-time jobs. Professional surfers are in the enviable position of getting paid to travel the world to go surfing. Leading the way on this path is Floridian Kelly Slater. Within professional surfing there's Kelly Slater and then there's everybody else.

Slater has won six world titles, more than any surfer on the planet. Now 30, he has spent the last few years in semiretirement and recently announced plans to start competing full-time again. During his time off he entered select events and managed to solidify his reputation as a world-class big-wave surfer by winning the "Quiksilver in memory of Eddie Aikau" contest in 20- to 25-foot waves at Waimea Bay in Hawaii.

A few miles up from Waimea Bay is the fabled Pipeline, the world famous wave known for its perfectly shaped tubes. The most prestigious surf contest in the world, the annual Pipeline Masters, is held there. Slater has won it five times.

KELLY SLATER IN ACTION AT THE
BILLABONG PRO ON JEFFREYS BAY IN
SOUTH AFRICA ON JULY 18, 2002.

The Pipeline Masters is held every winter with as much as $150,000 in total prize money at stake. The waves break close enough to shore to enable spectators to hear the roar and hiss of the sometimes 25-foot high breakers. The waves at Pipeline break in very shallow water over a sharp lava-rock reef. Leaving little room for error, this incredibly dangerous surf spot is for experienced surfers only. Even the best surfers in the world run into trouble at Pipeline, where broken boards and injuries are commonplace.

Surfing Pipeline for the first time is a definite rite of passage for any surfer. The only thing possibly more intimidating than the wave is the menacing crowd of local surfers. It takes years to work your way up the pecking order before you can gain even the slightest bit of respect there. The competition is fierce and just getting one good wave on a crowded day at Pipeline is a huge accomplishment. This is because there are usually only a few waves in comparison to the massive amount of surfers all jockeying for position. But all it takes is being at the right place at the right time to get the ride of your life.

Once you manage to catch a wave at Pipeline, the next challenge is negotiating the vertical drop-in while simultaneously standing up on your board. Then, depending on the shape of the wave, you might end up in the tube immediately.

But sometimes you need to work a little harder to get inside. Usually this means either slowing down by shifting your weight onto your back foot or speeding up by positioning yourself high on the wave and putting more weight on your front foot.

Experienced Pipeline surfers like Gerry Lopez make all this look smooth and effortless. Though it might seem safer and easier to take off on the shoulder at Pipeline, Lopez recommends taking off deeper behind the peak. He claims this allows you to get in earlier before the wave gets too steep and gives you more time to set up for the tube.

Another way to set up early for the tube at any spot is getting towed in by a jet ski. This has revolutionized surfing by allowing tow-in surfers like Laird Hamilton to successfully ride waves as big as 100 feet.

Hamilton is developing a new twist on tow-in surfing called foiling. By attaching a hydrofoil plane to the bottom of his tow-in board, Hamilton can glide two feet above the water; he compares the sensation to flying.

Hamilton believes the foil is the most efficient wave-riding instrument available to date; however, he also realizes it's still in its infancy stages design-wise. "To put the foil on giant waves is a lot to handle," he says. "We've ridden waves probably upwards of 20 feet at a bunch of different spots and it's hairball. But the future is wide open for creativity because it's just the beginning. The obvious direction I want to go is designing foils for riding giant waves."

Fortunately, Hamilton's achievements in surfing give him the financial freedom to avoid the 9-to-5 rat race, so he won't need to kill any innocent ants when the waves get "giant."

—*Gabe Sullivan*

Gabe Sullivan is a Laguna Beach, California, based freelance writer who has written for Surfer *magazine for nine years. He first surfed Pipeline in 1994 and caught two waves.*

New Heights

There's a revolution igniting the sport of skiing—and your parents have nothing to do with it. Once thought of as an activity for stodgy rich people, skiing is quickly becoming the coolest sport on snow. Instead of migrating to snowboarding, thousands of kids have taken new equipment, thrown out all the rules, and reinvented the sport.

Today's young skiers are catching bigger air, executing far more complex tricks, and bombing monstrous mountain faces faster than their single-plank brethren. And this transformation has all happened in five short years. The biggest factor contributing to the resurgence of skiing is equipment, "twin-tip" and "fat" skis specifically, and a handful of forward thinkers. In 1997 Canadian superstar skier Mike Douglas made a video promoting the twin-tip ski concept (one with a turned-up tail that can land tricks and ski backward, or "switch") and the myriad snowboard-influenced tricks he and his team developed during the 1995-1996 season.

Knowing that Japan was more willing than North America to accept a radical idea like this, Douglas sent the video to his friend, Japanese national freestyle coach Steve Fearing. Fearing shopped the idea around Japan and, in no time, ski manufacturing giant Salomon embraced the idea. The outcome: the groundbreaking Salomon 1080, the first true, functional, mass-produced twin-tip ski.

Douglas, coach of the Canadian Freestyle Team, had assembled a dream team of new-school skiers. The ensemble quickly became known as The New Canadian Air Force (the original Canadian Air Force was a notorious group of aerial skiers in the eighties known for flips and twists). J. F. Cusson, J. P. Auclair, Vincent Dorion, Shane Szocs, and Douglas began mastering techniques once thought reserved for snowboarders. They boosted out of halfpipes, spun tricks off 50-foot tabletop park jumps (often landing switch), and executed smooth rail slides. After a sleepy slump caused by neon clothes and a lack of innovation in the eighties and early nineties, skiing was about to become cool again. But only a handful of people knew it.

Around the time of Douglas' push in the freestyle realm, professional new-school skier Shane McConkey was working to develop a tool that would forever change big-mountain skiing (which is the common term for riding down the faces of large, powder-covered mountains). Until the early nineties skis were typically quite skinny, averaging about 65mm underfoot. While wider skis (more than 90mm underfoot) were used by middle-aged helicopter skiers, young hardcores wanted nothing to do with fat skis. Their use was considered cheating.

But not by McConkey. He realized that a fatter ski allowed him to ride on top of the powder rather than through it. This powerful, fast, smooth style of skiing looked

DOUGLAS CATCHES BIG AIR AT THE 1999 WINTER X
GAMES IN CRESTED BUTTE, COLORADO.

and felt more like surfing and snowboarding than skiing's typical slow, bobbing, pogo-stick motion.

In 1996, McConkey's ski sponsor, Volant, sent him a pair fat skis called Chubbs (today the skis would be considered mid-fats). Unlike all of the other expert skiers and pros, who thought fat skis were totally uncool and not a performance tool, McConkey gave them a try. He couldn't believe how it changed his skiing. Other pros, such as Brant Moles, also saw the advantages of fat skis and the trend snowballed. McConkey took the skis with him to every contest he entered and even brought them on-location for a film shoot. Only a year after he tried them—following McConkey's first landmark ski film appearance on fat skis in Matchstick Productions' *Fetish*—the industry awoke from its coma and started taking notice. A few simple innovations had changed everything.

Fast-forward a few years to today. Skiing has undergone one of the biggest and fastest overhauls in action-sports history. Every ski company now produces high-performance fat skis, twin-tips, and even hybrid "fat twin-tips" (these skis do it all: ski powder, park, and ride switch). Terrain parks, once reserved for snowboarders, are overrun by young, progressive skiers.

But perhaps the most important change revolves around the top athletes. After riders such as Douglas and McConkey paved the way, ski companies now embrace professional athletes, sponsoring them with contracts that range from small photo incentives to $50,000 annual salaries. Unlike professional snowboarders and surfers who got paid by their sponsors to appear in magazine photos

and film segments, skiers of the past who made it into similar media outlets were dirtbags funding their own hedonistic lifestyles. A photo in a magazine or a segment in a video was just a nice bonus—it didn't include a paycheck.

Today skiers are finally getting paid due to advertising campaigns that have done an about-face. Instead of utilizing lame product photos to sell equipment and clothing, the ski industry is following the other board sports' lead, using athletes' images to sell products.

To distinguish itself from skiing's old image, new-school skiing is called "freeskiing." Within freeskiing, there are two main camps: park and pipe trick skiers and big-mountain freeriders.

In 2001-2002, Tanner Hall, C. R. Johnson, Jon Olsson, Eric Pollard, Phil Belanger, and Candide Thovex made the biggest impacts on the park, pipe, and big-air scene. Hall, Johnson, and Olsson owned the podiums at the biggest contests of the year. Simply trading positions, the trifecta dominated the X Games, U.S. Open, and Red Bull Huck Fest. Pollard and Belanger were voted on and profiled by *Axis* magazine, the sport's newest and only all-freestyle mag, as the most influential riders of the year for their smooth styles and innovative technique.

At *Powder* magazine's Superpark 4—the premier park and pipe session of the year—Frenchman Thovex was unofficially crowned Skier of the Week by his fellow athletes. Thovex caught bigger air than anyone else, but the highlight came when he stomped a 110-foot, cork 5 tail grab (one of the hardest tricks) over the biggest hip jump built in 2002.

In the big-mountain arena, Seth Morrison, McConkey, Kent Kreitler, Jeremy Nobis, and Micah Black are the reigning leaders. These five athletes consistently produce stunning footage for the industry's best film segments by Matchstick Productions (MSP) and Teton Gravity Research. Of these five riders, Morrison is the standout leader. He took second place in *Powder* magazine's inaugural, Skier of the Year reader poll in 2002 and won Best Performance by a Male in the 2001 and 2002 *Powder* magazine Video Awards.

Morrison's accolades are earned through sweat and blood—literally. He is known for taking trick skiing typically reserved for the terrain park and incorporating it into high-speed descents down 3,000-foot Alaskan mountains. He's broken his nose more times than he can count while attempting to land backflips off 50-foot-plus cliffs.

Now 28, the flamboyant Morrison started skiing for MSP at 19 years old. After nearly a decade of pushing the sport to unforeseen levels, his life as the most influential and controversial big-mountain skier will come to life in the fall of 2002 in MSP's film biography, The Seth Morrison Chronicles.

With equipment at its technological apex, athletes utilizing the gear to push the sport beyond its perceived boundaries, and an industry finally stepping up to embrace the movement, skiing is poised to become the most exciting of all extreme sports. And while professional skiers and the industry have made astronomical changes to the sport in the last five years, the evolution has only just begun.

Tricks that seem complex now and speed records that appear unbreakable will soon be surpassed. The sport of yesterday that your parents remember won't be recognizable tomorrow. Forget what you've heard; skiing is rolling like an avalanche and there's nothing anyone can do to stop it.

—*Keith Carlsen*

Keith Carlsen is a freelance writer based in Salt Lake City, where he skis about 100 days a year, and the former editor of Powder *magazine.*

Upward Mobility

Sport climbing came into its own in the eighties, when people started focusing more on climbing style and performance rather than summiting by any means necessary. The essence of sport climbing is maintaining graceful movement over the rock while simultaneously pushing the performance envelope.

Sport climbing routes offer a safer environment to practice finessing hard moves without having to worry about hauling up a cumbersome load of gear. In traditional climbing, the leader often has to tinker with equipment in the middle of hard sections or risk running it out to easier territory.

Sport routes are typically bolted, which enables the use of lightweight, easy-to-place, quick-draw devices. This allows a climber to focus more on improving his or her performance--a definite plus since few climbers have the skill and confidence to place removable protective gear while climbing at their full physical potential.

The most common rating system used in rock climbing is called the Yosemite Decimal System, with the easiest climbs starting at 5.0 and the hardest currently rated at 5.15. During the middle to late seventies 5.11s were considered incredible. Then throughout the eighties 5.13s became the top-end standard.

By the early nineties 5.14s were the new threshold, and that's where high-performance climbing hit its ceiling. That is until recently,

when Chris Sharma broke the 5.15 barrier in the south of France with a route he named "Realization." It was a huge accomplishment, since prior to that 5.15 was considered not humanly possible within climbing circles.

Sharma, 21, started climbing in his home town of Santa Cruz, California, a region known more for producing professional surfers than climbing prodigies. Nonetheless, at 11 years old he told his father, Bob Sharma, that he was going to grow up to be a professional rock climber.

"The thing that makes him so unique," Tom Davis, cofounder and co-owner of Pacific Edge Climbing Gym in Santa Cruz, told Metroactive.com, "is that besides being exceptionally nice, he is completely unattached to the outcome of his every move. He is totally present with the move he's doing. Normally, a person feels afraid to make a move. He goes for it without fear."

Incredibly talented yet tastefully understated, Sharma seems more interested in talking about the experience of climbing rather than ratings, breakthroughs, or victories. "I love climbing," said Sharma. "It's a great way to be in nature. It's about moving on rock. It's not just a physical thing; it's also a spiritual thing . . . where time stops. You stop thinking about stuff. There is no past, present, or future. It all disintegrates."

While Sharma is the sport's golden child of the moment, female climber Lynn Hill is a proven veteran who is perhaps the most recognized woman rock climber in the world. In 1979 Hill made the first ascent of Ophir Broke, a 5.12/13a climb in Colorado that ranked as the hardest route ever done by a woman at the time.

In 1991 she climbed the first 5.14a ever achieved by a woman, a climb in Cimai, France, called Masse Critique. In 1992 she became the first person to complete a free ascent of "The Nose" route on El Capitan in Yosemite. She followed this feat by going back the next year and free-climbing "The Nose" again, but this time in less than 24 hours.

After a win or place in nearly every sport-climbing competition she entered in the eighties, Hill retired from the professional indoor sport-climbing circuit. Since then she's been traveling the world on mountain climbing expeditions. "I still feel that the most important part of climbing is having fun with your friends," she says, "and usually in a beautiful place, because rock climbing occurs in a natural environment. That's the real spirit of climbing."

Perhaps Hill's longevity as climbing's foremost female ambassador is due to her realization that the spirit of climbing isn't about competition or showing off for the camera, but about being outside surrounded by nature and sharing the experience with friends. However, she didn't achieve such notoriety in climbing by just hanging out in nature with her friends. She dedicates herself to the climbing discipline and plays by the rules.

And what exactly are the rules? Rule number one is safety. Reckless risk-taking is totally optional and climbing can be as safe as you choose to make it. Beyond safety, there are also some established rules of play commonly used by climbers. These fall into three categories: on-sight, flash, and redpoint.

Your on-sight level is the hardest route you can climb on your first try, without falls. You must do the climb without any prior coaching for it to be considered a true on-sight. If someone tells you how to do any of the moves prior to doing the climb, your first-try ascent will be considered a "flash." You only get one try to on-sight or flash a route.

If you require more than one attempt on the route, you'll be going for the redpoint, which means doing the climb from bottom to top without falls. Once you make it all the way to the top without falling you have redpointed the route. But whether you on-sight, flash, or redpoint, the most important rule to remember—besides always being safe—is to make sure you're always having fun.

—*Gabe Sullivan*

Gabe Sullivan is a Laguna Beach, California, based freelance writer whose work has appeared in Surfer *magazine,* Snowboarder *magazine,* Men's Journal, *and* Rolling Stone.

LYNN HILL

A Free Nation

Professional freerider Robbie Bourdon floats 30 feet above the earth. No less than 25 still, video, and film cameras point directly at his compact, 5'4" body, all hoping to catch a piece of history in the making. It's October 2001, at the finals of the Red Bull Rampage in Virgin, Utah—North America's first-ever freeride mountain bike contest (judged on style, fluidity, control, and line choice rather than as a timed race).

After the qualifying round, Bourdon sits in second place by four points. He knows it will take a huge maneuver like this monster air to win the contest. But after he slams down on his target--a narrow piece of singletrack--he collides with a small bush that rips him off his intended line and catapults him toward the edge of a 50-foot cliff. When he comes to a stop he's dangling over the cliff's edge. With his bike clutched in his right hand, four bystanders grab him and hoist the rider back to flat ground.

Instead of giving up, Bourdon immediately returns to the top of the cliff drop that almost ruined him. "I felt like an idiot not landing it, because I'd already done it three times in practice, no problem," Bourdon said later of the ill-fated jump. "I just thought, 'What the hell happened?' I said I had to do it again because I just had to."

On his second attempt, he pedaled with furious speed onto the take-off ramp, boosted into the air, glided for several seconds, and, this time, cleanly stuck the landing. En route to the finish line, he dropped a 10-foot air into a smooth, sinuous carve as onlookers stared dumbfounded. Welcome to new-school mountain biking at its finest.

Bourdon's air—and the frightening antics of 21 other freeriders invited to the Rampage—was the culmination of 10 years of freeride mountain biking's evolution. Freeriding's unofficial official birthplace was Kamloops, British Columbia, its forefathers a small group of aliens known as Richie Schley, Brett Tippie, and Craig Olsson.

After an intense BMX affair waned, Schley (who won the Canadian BMX title in 1993) and childhood friends Tippie and Olsson turned to mountain bikes. But due to their rural and lawless Canadian surroundings, mountain biking quickly became something different for this trio. Sure, riding smooth singletrack was fun and all, but these guys vibrated on a different level. They jonesed for something bigger and more exciting.

After dabbling in downhill shuttles, the riders eventually turned to the endless, eroded clay bluffs and ridges that reached 3,000 feet above their town. On these trails and wide-open faces (imagine a field of backcountry powder covered in smooth dirt), they could ride however and wherever they wanted. Early freeride lines in Kamloops earned infamous names such as "The Scar" and "The Razorbacks" for their promise of

ROBBIE BOURDON

severe consequences in the case of a crash.

And crash violently they did. Eventually, though, through much trial and a lot of error, Schley, Tippie, and Olsson got really good. Their radical descents, technical lines, and stylish airs attracted the attention of the industry's biggest filmmakers and magazines. In 1995 the triumvirate starred in the

groundbreaking, controversial, first-ever freeride mountain bike film, *Pulp Traction*. In 1997 the boys were featured in a 10-page article in *Bike* magazine (the only publication willing to embrace this debated discipline at the time), simply entitled, "Sick."

In the article, writer Leslie Anthony summed up the scene. "Radical freeriding. No trails. Descending natural terrain. Man against mountain. Many say it's the next horizon for mountain biking. And while [Schley, Tippie, and Olsson] may be ground zero for the start of the revolution, they're the first to admit they're no heroes, that what they're doing isn't all that unique, and that this kind of thing is probably being played out, at least on some level, in a hundred local scenes around the continent."

The boys from Kamloops were spot-on with their observations. By the mid-nineties, freeriding exploded. Bike manufacturers who'd developed full-suspension bikes for downhill racing made minor tweaks to design and invented a brand new category. Freeride bikes—with big tires, cushy front and rear suspension, riser bars, and disc brakes--were designed to go really fast downhill, but also have the ability to climb (unlike a dedicated downhill bike).

Not without resistance from environmentalists and purists alike, freeriding flourished. For mountain bikers who'd ridden for a decade, the redesigned bikes opened up a new world with faster speeds, bigger air than once thought possible, and most importantly, loads of wide-eyed fun. A subculture followed—one with baggy clothing, pierced bodies, and bleached hair. Today freeriding and its disciples are ubiquitous. It's the hottest and most exciting genre of mountain biking to both participate in and watch.

Since *Pulp Traction*, more than a dozen freeride movies have hit the scene. The most influential was the *Kranked* series by filmmaker Christian Begin, who filmed a great deal for *Pulp*. Today filmmaker Derek Westerlund's *New World Disorder* series has taken the torch and run wild. In print media it's impossible to open one of the bike industry's major magazines and not see a shot of some freerider boosting sky-high off a dirt jump or performing some death-defying urban stunt.

With the media's support freeriders have entered a world once reserved for surfers and skateboarders--the one with a paycheck. Similar to freeskiing's early days, nonracing mountain bikers weren't paid like surfers and skaters are. But that is changing. Mountain biking is developing heroes outside of racing. While forefathers Schley and Tippie are still heavily involved with the scene (Schley is by far the most published freerider in history), there is an army of ripping young kids taking over.

Fifteen-year-old Kyle Straight is the quintessential example of the next generation. With a BMX and dirt-jumping background, Straight made a big splash in the downhill racing scene before exploding as a freerider. At the Rampage freeride competition, Straight was the most talked-about rider. While earning his ninth-place finish, spectators pointed in disbelief as the then 14-year-old dropped the same, incredibly steep lines as competitors 10 years his senior. Among those competitors was Wade Simmons, another Canadian badass who's arguably the best freeride mountain biker in the world today.

And then there was 20-year-old Robbie Bourdon—going for broke in the finals, hucking his carcass off a 30-foot cliff, nearly crushing himself, and returning for more. While Bourdon's bold moves overshadowed much of the competition's action, he couldn't beat out fellow countryman Simmons for the championship. Bourdon took third, but more importantly, he sealed his reputation as mountain biking's big-air maven.

One month later Bourdon had a full-page magazine ad from eyewea and clothing company sponsor Oakley. Shortly thereafter, Red Bull picked him up as a team rider.

While it took nearly a decade, it seems the esoteric sport of freeride mountain biking has reached critical mass. Professional riders are being paid for their abilities. Mortal riders, who once thought cruising groomed singletrack was the ultimate mountain biking experience, are boosting air and riding faster than ever imagined.

Freeriding is tangible evidence of the evolutionary process. Once a quiet, peaceful sport, mountain biking has evolved into a big-hit, power-hungry discipline with sponsored athletes, media appeal, and no end in sight.

—Keith Carlsen

Keith Carlsen is a Utah-based freelance writer who contributes stories and photographs to Bike, Outside, Powder, Axis, Hooked on the Outdoors, *and numerous other magazines and action-sports publications. He also skis and bikes way too much.*

KYLE STRAIGHT